BATTLE OVER SUSSEX

Pat Burgess
Andy Saunders

MP Middleton Press

Cover pictures -

Left. A plentiful harvest .... 1940 style! Unteroffizier Leo Zaunbrecher's Messerschmitt 109, down amongst the corn stooks at Selmeston on 12th August 1940, attracts the gaze of inquisitive villagers.

Right. These two Hurricane pilots of 249 Squadron died within hours of each other over Sussex on 27th September 1940. Pilot Officer J.R.B. Meaker (on the left) was killed over Dallington in the afternoon when he baled out but his parachute failed to open. Meaker, although born Co. Cork, had his home in Sussex, was educated at Chichester High School and later became a reporter on the Chichester Observer. Flying Officer R.F. Burton died in a heroic action over Hailsham when, apparently out of ammunition, he rammed his opponent from the sky.

First reprint August 1990
Second reprint June 1991
Third reprint July 1993
Fourth reprint February 1995
Fifth reprint August 1995
Sixth reprint June 1999
Seventh reprint March 2003

ISBN 0 906520 79 7

© Middleton Press, 1990

Design   Deborah Esher
Typesetting   Barbara Mitchell

Published by
 Middleton Press
 Easebourne Lane
 Midhurst, West Sussex
 GU29 9AZ
Tel: 01730 813169
Fax: 01730 812601

Printed & bound by Biddles Ltd,
 Guildford and Kings Lynn

CONTENTS

4	Acknowledgments and Authors notes
4	RAF and Luftwaffe organisation 1940
6	RAF Tangmere
9	Ford Aerodrome
10	Map of Chichester area
11	Map of Brighton area
12	Map of Eastbourne area
13	Map of Wadhurst area
14	Arundel Municipal Borough
15	Battle Rural District
20	Bexhill Municipal Borough
23	Bognor Regis Urban District
25	Brighton County Borough
28	Burgess Hill Urban District
29	Chailey Rural District
33	Chanctonbury Rural District
37	Chichester Municipal Borough
39	Chichester Rural District
51	Cuckfield Rural District
53	Cuckfield Urban District
54	Eastbourne County Borough
61	East Grinstead Urban District
62	Hailsham Rural District
66	Hastings County Borough
68	Horsham Rural District
70	Horsham Urban District
71	Hove Municipal Borough
72	Lewes Municipal Borough
74	Littlehampton Urban District
77	Midhurst Rural District
78	Newhaven Urban District
78	Petworth Rural District
79	Portslade Urban District
79	Rye Municipal Borough
81	Seaford Urban District
81	Shoreham-by-Sea Urban District
82	Southwick Urban District
82	Uckfield Rural District
86	Worthing Municipal Borough
89	Worthing Rural District
93	Table of aircraft down in Sussex

Map of the administrative boundaries effective in 1940 and used throughout this book. The figures are the page numbers, listed above.

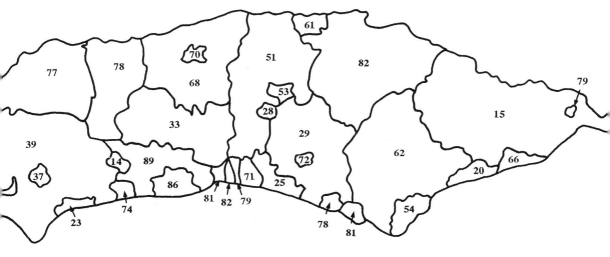

English Channel

ACKNOWLEDGEMENTS

Many good friends, fellow enthusiasts and historians have generously given of their time and expertise over the years during which this book has been in its research stage. Special thanks must therefore go to Alan Brown, Peter Cornwell, John Ellis, Peter Foote, Steve Hall, Phillipa Hodgkiss, Dennis Knight, Nigel Parker, Simon Parry, Mike Payne, Dr Alfred Price, Lionel Quinlan, Winston and Gordon Ramsey, George Tuke and Ken Wynn.

Much help was provided along the way by Richard King of the Ministry of Defence Air Historical Branch, staff of the Commonwealth War Graves Commission and German records offices in Berlin. Additionally, the county record offices in Chichester and Lewes have been helpful in providing access to local ARP and Civil Defence Reports whilst many local library reference sections have assisted in tracking down photographs and tracing additional information. Brian Bridges also deserves a special mention for his help in providing access to wartime police records for the county.

Last, but by no means least, we would both like to pay special tribute to our wives and families who have endured many years of an almost obsessive quest for both tangible and documentary material relating to 1940. Without them, this project would have been impossible.

AUTHOR'S NOTES

Documentary archive material from a wide range of sources has been drawn upon to build up a jigsaw type picture of aerial events in and over Sussex during 1940. Most important have been local police, ARP and Civil Defence reports which give the dates, times, locations and brief details of events. Married to official RAF records now held at the Public Record Office, Kew, and to reports filed with MOD's Air Historical Branch, it has thus been possible to compile a comprehensive listing of the losses of all aircraft in the county, including such details as crew names, serial numbers of the aircraft and combat data. In the context of this book it has only been possible to list the barest details of each event, although the authors have researched each incident thoroughly with every event being fully documented with contemporary material.

Restrictions which war brought with it in the form of travel restraints, a shortage of film, censorship and the Control of Photography Order 1939, created many difficulties when it came to retrospectively building up a photographic record of the period. Quite apart from these problems, the passage of fifty years has meant that whatever material did exist has been seriously depleted through loss or deliberate destruction, with a good many original prints and photographic negatives and plates being dumped by news agencies and photographers in the intervening years. Private source photographs are also rare, for the variety of reasons previously mentioned. It will also be noted that the vast majority of pictures reproduced here depict shot down German aircraft, with very few of British machines - despite the fact that a good many more British than German machines fell in the county! The reason for this is that most of these pictures were taken for reproduction in newspapers and periodicals and it was clearly detrimental to British morale to show pictures of downed RAF aircraft, the British Censorship Bureau thereby deliberately creating the impression that only enemy machines were being lost! Consequently pictures of crashed British fighters are rare in the extreme and those few which have been traced are all included. Also, it will be noted that the pictures appearing in these pages are predominantly of crashed aircraft and related subjects rather than of the effects of bombing etc. It was a conscious decision to bias the emphasis of our photographic content in this direction as this book is essentially a record of the Battle of Britain and to most people this conjures up images of aircraft crashing in cornfields, on downland and along country lanes! In any event, one picture of bombed rubble is much like another, although we have included such shots where it was felt the photograph was of sufficient interest or significance to warrant inclusion, or where no other photograph of reproducible quality exists for that particular geographical location. Finally, by way of explanation on the format of this book, it will be found that coverage is given to the entire county on a geographical basis using the boundaries of rural districts, urban districts, municipal boroughs and county boroughs then in being and laid out in alphabetical order throughout the book.

The authors would be interested in hearing from anyone with new information or photographs or from anyone who has memories or even souvenirs of shot down wartime aircraft in the county. They can be contacted via the Tangmere Military Aviation Museum, P.O. Box 50, Tangmere Airfield, Chichester, West Sussex, PO20 6ER.

MAPS

The maps shown on pages 10 to 13 are all based upon the 1933 edition of the Ordnance Survey of Great Britain. Four regions of the county have been selected to give a representative coverage of the East and West of Sussex on which has been marked a proportion of the aircraft down in those areas. For clarity not every aeroplane down in each area covered by the maps reproduced here has neccesarily been marked. Those that have been marked are indicated in the exact position when known, or at a close approximation to the believed or reported position of the crash. The size of the county and number of incidents logged precludes the inclusion of maps for the whole of Sussex marked with the three hundred or so crashes. The scale has been reduced to ¾" to 1 mile. The numbers shown on the maps are listed in the tables on pages 93 to 95.

PHOTOGRAPHS

Whilst every effort has been made to clear copyright, the sources of the pictures used are varied and, in many cases, obscure. Some are from private collections, whilst others originate from agencies and organisations no longer in existence. Consequently, the publication of pictures on which clearance has not been given is unintentional, but it is hoped that appearance within this book will be seen as a fitting tribute to those who participated in the Battle of Britain.

RAF ORGANISATION 1940

Whilst the organisation of RAF operational units into Squadrons will no doubt be familiar to most readers, it is perhaps worth explaining that each Squadron comprised roughly about

twelve aircraft and a corresponding number of pilots or aircrew. Clearly this number was subject to fluctuation depending upon serviceable aircraft and losses of pilots or machines. A Squadron could often be depleted to below strength pending the replacement of men or machines. However, the Battle Order of the RAF can be found elsewhere in other reference works, although it is worth mentioning here that the entire County of Sussex fell within the defence region of No. 11 Group, RAF Fighter Command.

LUFTWAFFE ORGANISATION 1940

The organisation of the German airforce and the official designation of its operational units will not be familiar to many readers and thus a brief explanation of such designations as used within the context of this book is appropriate.

German operational units were divided up into Geschwaders; a Geschwaders translating roughly into English as Squadron. However, the strength of a Geschwader was many times that of a Squadron, but it was sub-divided up into tactical units which more closely represented the strength of an RAF Squadron. Fighter units were Jagdgeschwaders (abbreviated to JG) and Bomber units were Kampfgeschwaders (abbreviated to KG). Within each Geschwader there could be up to five groups (Gruppen), each sub-divided up again into Staffeln, the nearest approximation to an RAF Squadron. Additionally, each Gruppe had its Staff Flight (Stab) of H.Q. Staff.

RAF AND LUFTWAFFE RANK EQUIVALENTS

Aircraftman (2)	(AC2)	(Fl)	Flieger
" (1)	(AC1)	(Gefr)	Gefreiter
Leading Aircraftmen	(LAC)	(Obgefr)	Obergefreiter
Corporal	(Cpl)		Hauptgefreiter
Sergeant	(Sgt)	(Uffz)	Unteroffizier/Unterfeldwebel
Flight Sergeant	(Flt Sgt)	(Fw)	Feldwebel
Warrant Officer	(WO)	(Oberfw)	Oberfeldwebel/Stabsfeldwebel
Pilot Officer	(Plt Off)	(Lt)	Leutnant
Flying Officer	(Fg Off)	(Oblt)	Oberleutnant
Flight Lieutenant	(Flt Lt)	(Hptm)	Hauptmann
Squadron Leader	(Sqn Ldr)		Major
Wing Commander	(Wg Cdr)		Oberstleutnant
Group Captain	(Gp Capt)		Oberst

The above is a list of approximate equivalents in rank of the two services although the opposites are necessarily speculative in some cases as no exact equivalent may always exist. In brackets the abbreviated version of the rank as used in this book is given as appropriate.

RAF TANGMERE

The single most important defence establishment in Sussex during 1940 was the RAF Fighter Command aerodrome at Tangmere. Owing its origins to an emergency landing by Royal Flying Corps pilot Geoffrey Dorman during 1916, Tangmere became a "Sector" station within the structure of Fighter Command. In other words, the principal station in one of the seven sectors of No.11 Group which defended the South and South East of England. In RAF parlance Tangmere was Sector Station "A".

During the 1920s and 30s it was the home of the sleek and elegant silver biplane fighters of No. 1 and 43 Squadrons, first of all Gloster Gamecocks, followed by Siskins and Hawker Furies. At this time, the airfield was laid down to grass, but with smart new brick-built buildings, a palatial officers mess, and good sports facilities, Tangmere became a sought after posting. In addition, the pursuits of golf, sailing and horse racing were all close at hand and the summer routine of compressing all flying into the morning and virtually closing the station down from 1pm made its attraction greater! In those halcyon days, the airfield became something akin to an exclusive club and yet it still became a symbol of excellence within the Royal Air Force, setting the highest standards and maintaining the enviable traditions of 1 and 43 Squadrons. However, those glorious days were not to last. War loomed.

Two runways of 1,600 X 50 yds were constructed N - S and NE - SW, blast protection pens built around a new perimeter track and the so recently camouflaged silver biplanes were replaced by a newer, sleeker breed of fighter: Hawker Hurricanes. In addition, Avro Ansons of 217 Squadron were based here but departed to a new home in Cornwall just prior to the outbreak of war. When war came, No. 1 Squadron was almost immediately posted to France, whilst No. 43 flew north to Acklington, leaving Tangmere to Blenheims of 92 Squadron, Hurricanes of 501 Squadron and Gladiators of 605 Squadron. Apart from its clear role in the defence of Britain, the station played no really active role over the next few months, although activity began to increase again with the fall of France during the Spring of 1940 and the eventual return of Nos 1 and 43 Squadrons prior to the Battle of Britain.

During July of 1940, the opening month of that battle, Tangmere's fighter squadrons now numbered four - 1, 43, 145 and 601; all of them flying Hurricanes. During this month all these squadrons were involved in the regular skirmishes with the Luftwaffe over the Channel, resulting in numerous successes but, sadly, also the inevitable losses. Meanwhile a "satellite" airfield was being prepared just down the road at Westhampnett and was ready for occupancy by 145 Squadron on 8th August. Today, Westhampnett airfield survives as Goodwood Airfield, unlike its parent station, Tangmere, which was almost wiped out of existence on 16th August 1940! On this day, at precisely 1pm, a large force of Junkers Ju.87 dive bombers screamed out of the sun in a devastating attack which left many dead and injured, two hangars destroyed and numerous other buildings hit or damaged. In addition, six Blenheims, seven Hurricanes, one Magister and at least one Spitfire were destroyed - along with a number of cars and other vehicles. Nevertheless, in spite of all the mayhem the Station Operations Record stated that: "The depressing situation was dealt with in an orderly manner and it is considered that the traditions of the RAF were upheld by all ranks. It must be considered that the major attack launched on this station was a victory for the RAF". Indeed so, for a good number of the raiders were shot down in the immediate locality by Tangmere based fighters, and the intervention of these Hurricanes may well have disrupted the attack to the extent that even worse damage was prevented. Sadly, whilst the attack was in progress, Pilot Officer Billy Fiske of 601 Squadron crash-landed his burning Hurricane on the cratered airfield but succumbed to his injuries the next day in hospital at Chichester. Even after the destruction of 16th August 1940, Tangmere was never non - operational for even one single hour and continued throughout the remainder of the Battle in the forefront of Britain's defence. Indeed, the majority of enemy aircraft downed in Sussex were claimed by Tangmere based squadrons and many of its own aircraft were amongst those lost in the county. Today, the beautifully kept St.

1. Looking south, this post-war aerial shot of Tangmere shows clearly the main runways and perimeter tracks, together with the hangars and buildings. The A27 can be seen running east-west at the northern boundary.

Andrews Churchyard at Tangmere bears testimony to the ferocity of those 1940 battles; the graves of RAF airmen side-by-side with those of their enemies.

Into 1941 the fighter squadrons went on the offensive, taking the air war to enemy occupied France in the form of fighter "sweeps". The Tangmere Wing was, at this time, led by the legendary legless pilot, Wing Commander Douglas Bader, but, in August 1941, Bader was brought down over France and captured. Nevertheless, the fighting sprit engendered during 1940 and into 1941 flourished, and Tangmere remained an important link in the chain of defensive airfields. It became a base for nightfighters, and later Whirlwind, Typhoon and Mustang aircraft, subsequently playing a vital role in the Dieppe raid on 19th August 1942 and D-Day invasions of 6th June,

1944, when its Squadrons provided air cover over the beachheads. But Tangmere's history was not exclusively fighter orientated.

Apart from the frequent arrival at night of crippled or disabled bombers flying home from raids deep inside Europe, there were other nocturnal comings and goings at Tangmere. Black painted Lysander aircraft made clandestine night time departures ferrying agents and members of the Special Operations Executive into and out of France, landing by moonlight and torchlight in fields right under the noses of the Germans! These highly secret flights were naturally shrouded in great mystery and Tangmere Cottage, opposite the airfield gates, became the base from where the agents were prepared for their flights or debriefed on return.

Post-war there was something of an

7

anti-climax from the drama of the preceding five years, but in 1945, the Fighter Leaders School was based here and Douglas Bader returned! Into the jet age the Meteor fighters now replaced their familiar piston engine forbears. A new World Airspeed Record was established off the Sussex Coast by Group Captain Donaldson in a specially prepared Meteor during 1946, a speed of 616 mph being attained. However, Tangmere remained part of the Air Defence UK network despite the fact that, yet again, the World Air Speed Record was claimed from here. Squadron Leader Neville Duke reached 727 mph in a Hawker Hunter during 1953 and later this type of jet was based at Tangmere with operational fighter squadrons. Gradually, however, Tangmere's place in the UK defence strategy diminished and it took on significantly less important and exciting roles until, in 1970, the station was finally closed down. Handed over to the Department of Environment's Property Services Agency, the once immaculate and proud airfield declined into decay. The Spitfire gate guardian was taken away and the

RAF ensign lowered for the very last time over this historic site. Rapidly the airfield and its buildings fell victim to theft, vandalism and nature before the flying field itself was sold off for agricultural use, the hangars converted to grain stores for the EEC Intervention Board and the buildings sold for eventual demolition and development as housing estates and light industrial usage. Mindful that the memory of this place and those who flew, fought and died from here should never be forgotten, the Tangmere Military Aviation Museum Trust was set up in 1982. There is now a thriving museum, the two authors of this book having both played a significant part in its establishment. As less and less of the airfield remains to show what once had been, it is encouraging that something survives to tell the future generations about Tangmere.

This field as famed as Agincourt,
Or Crecy, with their mailed hosts,
Where those who valued freedom fought,
Stands guarded by its valiant ghosts.

May the sacrifices made by those airmen in the service of their respective countries and the scale of civilian loss of life resulting from aerial warfare over the county not be quickly or carelessly forgotten. This book is a tribute to all who suffered.
   ANDY SAUNDERS & PAT BURGESS, 1990

3.   Shaken service personnel emerge from their slit trenches after the last of the bombs had fallen from a raiding force of Junkers 87 Stuka dive bombers at Ford aerodrome on 18th August 1940. Smoke rises from burning buildings, hangars and fuel stores.

4.   Casting a black shroud across the summer sky, Ford aerodrome blazes after the raid. Seventeen aircraft were wrecked, twenty eight personnel killed and seventy five wounded, one of the most serious death-tolls resulting from Luftwaffe raids on British airfields. →

2.   Smoke and flames rise from the bomb blasted hangars at Tangmere following the awesome attack by Junkers 87 Stuka dive bombers on 16th August 1940.

FORD AERODROME

Whilst the origins of Ford as an aerodrome go back to 1917, its role in the Battle of Britain was comparatively insignificant, although the Luftwaffe apparently did not share this view and singled it out for a devastating attack on 18th August 1940. In fact, the airfield housed only Fleet Air Arm training squadrons, aircraft repair facilities and several stored aircraft. At this time it was a Royal Naval Air Station, officially known as HMS Peregrine, but the raid was the end, temporarily, of Naval occupation. In any event, the FAA had already recognised as fool-hardy the siting of a training airfield in a "combat" area and had been in the process of withdrawing, the events of 18th August 1940, precipitating the final withdrawal. Ironically, if the Luftwaffe supposed that they were denying the RAF an operational airfield the opposite was the case! On 30th September 1940, HMS Peregrine was paid off and Ford became RAF Station Ford, 11 Group, Fighter Command. During the Battle of Britain, though, it played no key or significant role in the air defence of the United Kingdom, but later it was to come into its own. Fighters, night fighters, bombers and fighter bombers were based here and it played an important part in the Dieppe and D-Day operations, but it was as a night fighter base that Ford seemed to excel. Post war, the Navy returned with Ford becoming HMS Peregrine once again on 1st August 1945, housing Fleet Air Arm fighter units up until its final decommissioning on 13th November 1958, when the site was returned to agricultural use and some of the buildings became an open prison.

Although having had an interesting and varied use in its time as an airfield it was, nevertheless, not to acheive the same degree of international public fame or popularity amongst those stationed there as did its more illustrious neighbour, Tangmere.

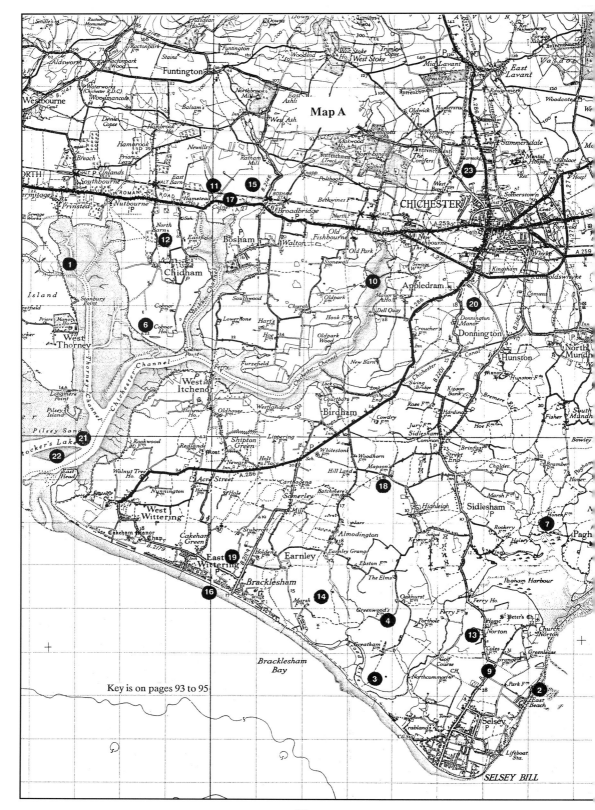

Map A

Key is on pages 93 to 95

Map B

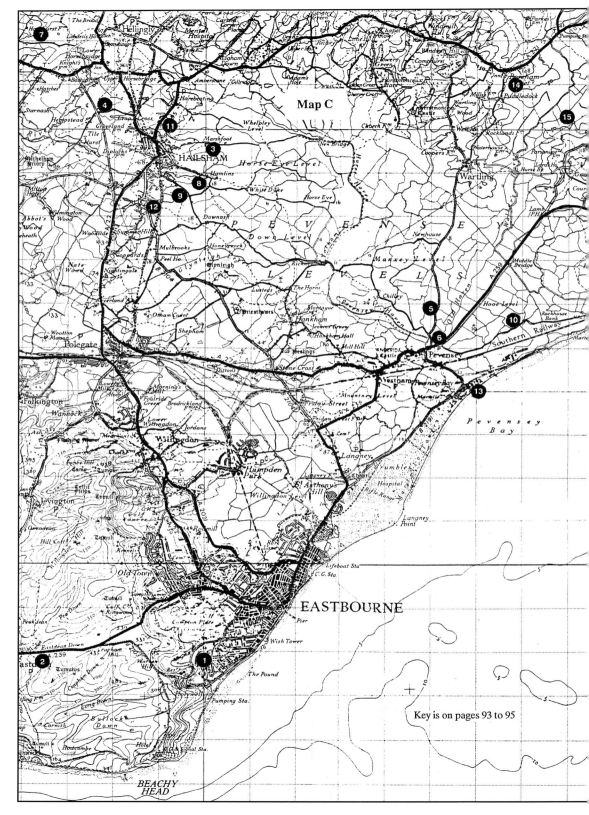

Map C

Key is on pages 93 to 95

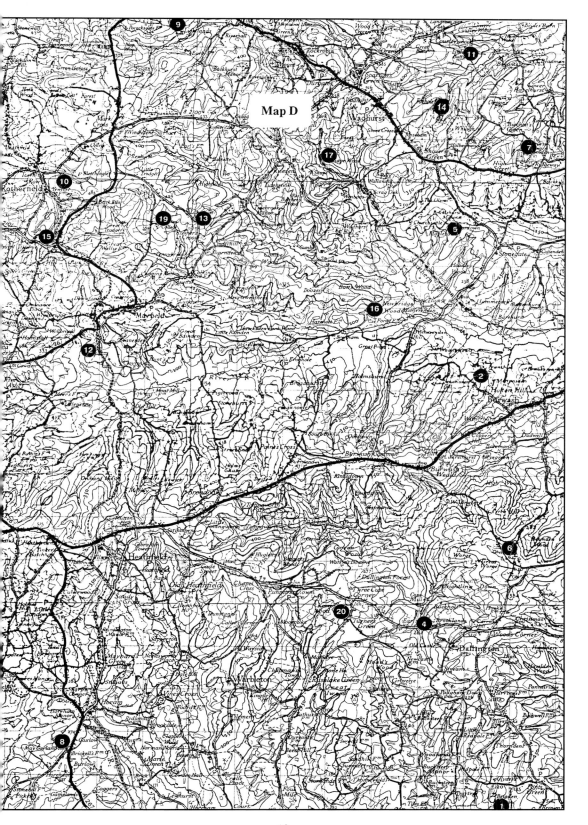

Map D

ARUNDEL MUNICIPAL BOROUGH

5-6. On 13th August 1940, the destruction of war came to Swanbourne Lake, Arundel. A Junkers 88 became a victim of the Luftwaffe's "Eagle Day" and smashed itself to pieces on hitting the trees above the west bank cascading into the lake. Little remained as these soldiers picked over the wreckage.

Despite its close proximity to the airfields of Ford and Tangmere, the almost constant aerial activity and the enormous variety of missiles and weapons which fell in the borough, not one of its citizens may be found on the UK Civilian War Dead Roll for the entire duration of the war. However, 1940 saw its moments of drama and excitement for Arundel, the most noteworthy day being the crash of a Junkers Ju88 bomber into Swanbourne Lake on 13th August 1940. Shot down by Tangmere based Hurricanes whilst en-route to bomb Farnborough, the aeroplane struck the beech trees on the west side of the lake, tearing itself apart as it tumbled down the steep embankment. Striking the footpath, the engines tore themselves out of what remained of the airframe, the rest of the fragmented wreckage cascading down into the lake itself, where one of the mainwheel landing tyres floated on a sheen of aviation spirit. Of the crew of four, two baled out to become prisoners of war, these being Oberlt. Rose and Uffz. Scholz. Fw. Bickel's parachute fouled the tailplane, dragging him to his death, whilst Hptm. Strauch was found in a tree, mortally wounded. Fifty years on, the massive trees which still bore the scars of the crashing Junkers had all been felled by the October 1987 storm. However, in 1989 the lake dried out, revealing once again evidence of the event, when portions of the aircraft emerged from the mud on the bed of the lake. Amongst the wreckage, an unexploded 50kg bomb came to light, being detonated by No.33 Explosive Ordnance Disposal, Royal Engineers, on 3rd November 1989 - a potent reminder of wartime days in Sussex! Subsequently, during the early part of 1990, further bombs were found at the site by an RAF Bomb Disposal team, one 50 kg bomb and two 250 kg bombs being discovered and de-fused.

BATTLE RURAL DISTRICT

As one of the largest rural districts, Battle had the highest proportion of crashed aircraft within its boundaries, a total of 67 falling there, within the timescale covered by this book. Today when surveying the peaceful pastoral landscape of "1066 Country" it is difficult to envisage the scenes which would have been enacted here on this very spot where William and Harold had met in deadly conflict if the outcome of the Battle of Britain had been different. Had that conflict not been won then, it is very likely that elements of the German Sixteenth Army's No. VII Corps, or General Guderian's Panzer tanks, would have been doing battle with perhaps the Devonshire Regiment and Home Guard on the field of Senlac.

Although the value of bland statistics may be arguable, it is, nevertheless, sobering to see the scale of warfare which came to Battle Rural District. In total there were 2,472 "alerts" (air raid warnings), 989 incidents, 30 civilian fatalities with 75 severely injured and 249 slightly injured casualties. In addition, damage to property resulted in the total loss of 166 habitations, with a staggering 8,282 other properties damaged to a greater or lesser degree. But all this carnage and mayhem was not without cost to the Luftwaffe.

One of the first losses to the enemy in the Battle District was a Messerschmitt Bf110 shot down at School Farm, Hooe, during the early evening of 15th August 1940 whilst returning from an infamous yet ill-fated raid on Croydon which cost the attacking unit (Erp.Gr.210) its Commanding Officer and seven aircraft and crews. (See also Uckfield Rural District). The aeroplane down at Hooe was landed virtually intact by its pilot, Ltn.Karl-Heinz Koch, after an attack by a Biggin Hill based Hurricane of 32 Squadron flown by Flt. Lt.H.a'B.Russell. Koch, his units Technical Officer, was taken prisoner and conveyed to Battle Abbey for temporary incarceration by the Devonshire Regt. whilst his badly wounded gunner, Uffz.Kahl, was taken off to hospital. Koch endured the remainder of the war years as a POW, whilst Kahl was repatriated due to his serious injuries. Their Messerschmitt, meanwhile, had been shipped off to the USA for technical evaluation by the Northrop Aeroplane Company.

Prior to this, the first German loss in the area, a near disaster had befallen No. 3 Squadron when five of their Hurricanes had made emergency landings in the Dallington area. En-route from Manston to Croydon on 10th September 1939, the Squadron encountered low cloud and very poor visibility, obliging five aeroplanes to land around Dallington. None of the pilots were hurt, and although some of the Hurricanes suffered minor damage in this episode at least two were able to be flown out later.

With the Battle of Britain in full swing by September 1940, it was inevitable that the wreckages of British machines would litter the countryside alongside the carcasses of German ones. Fortunately, many of the RAF pilots survived their ordeal to fly and fight another day. Such a survivor was Sgt.G.A.Whipps, a Spitfire pilot with the Westhampnett based 602 Squadron. September 6th 1940 saw him in action above East Sussex when he was shot down in a brief skirmish with Messerschmitt 109s. Taking to his parachute, Whipps landed close to his wrecked Spitfire on Pelsham Farm, Peasmarsh, where farm worker Dick Moore was first on the scene. Whipps was struggling with his parachute and having difficulty in retaining his balance on the heavy clods of soil as the canopy billowed in the breeze. To assist him Dick Moore stood on the 'chute. As he helped, Whipps asked for a cigarette, but Dick recalled how useless he felt when he told him that he had left them at the farm; "Here was this poor chap shot out of the sky defending his country and I couldn't even give him a fag! "

British losses, of course, were to continue, but on 11th September three Heinkel HeIII bombers came to grief in the area. Two came down close together at Broomhill, East Guldeford, their crews setting fire to the impotent bombers and sending columns of thick black smoke into the blue sky, contrasting with the tangled white vapour trails high above. The third Heinkel ended up at Gate Farm,

Staplecross, where it blew up shortly after crashing.

Sunday, 15th September, was a busy day too. A Dornier 17 ended its days at Eighteen Pounder Farm, Westfield, shot down by a Spitfire flown by Fg.Off.Michael Staples of 609 Squadron. As it arced out across the sea before turning in for its final landing, one of the crew took to his parachute and drifted down into the Channel where he presumably drowned. No trace of him was ever found, but his three colleagues were luckier and survived their subsequent crash landing. In the same battle, Squadron Leader George Denholm, CO of 603 Sqn, was obliged to abandon his Spitfire over Fairlight as his aeroplane thumped into the cliff top at Warren Farm, the severed Rolls-Royce Merlin engine continued under its own momentum over the cliff edge crashing onto the beach below.

The vicious fighting of September continued on into October and on the 25th of that month a Messerschmitt 109 was sent flaming from a dog fight just north of Hastings, and plunged vertically at full throttle into a drainage ditch on Lower Lidham Hill Farm, Guestling, where it vanished from sight. All that remained to show an aeroplane had passed this way was a gash in the embankment, a few pathetic shards of metal strewn about and one of the mainwheel tyres. The pilot, Fw.Willi Koslowski, had baled out with serious burns and landed by parachute in an adjacent field, where he was tended to by off duty Nurse Baker. Rolling him into a ditch to escape machine gun bullet raining down from the battle above, Koslowski muttered his appreciation to Nurse Baker, "Fraulein Güt" he kept repeating whilst the assembling group of onlookers continually derided her efforts,

suggesting that perhaps she should instead let him die. Koslowski did not die and was eventually taken away on a makeshift stretcher provided by the ladder from a fire engine. Later, Nurse Baker received a thank you letter from Koslowski in his POW Camp in which he told her that she would receive a commendation from Hitler once the war had been won! Victor of the battle in which Koslowski was downed was a Sussex man from Midhurst, Sgt.Pilot Raymond Gent of 501 Squadron flying a Hurricane, and who fired 1,200 rounds at 200 yards in a ten second burst. In his official report, Gent speaks of the "inside of the cockpit..... a mass of flames" and that the crash occurred approximately three to four miles north of Hastings. Undoubtedly, this was the machine which fell at Guestling and in 1989 wreckage was recovered from a depth of over 30ft by a team from the Tangmere Military Aviation Museum. The engine was still in fine condition, preserved in peat and clay, whilst the tail section bore testimony to Gent's shooting, riddled with .303 bullet holes.

The Battle of Britain drew to a sad conclusion in the Rural District for the defending forces when, on 30th October, Pilot Officer Hillary Edridge was shot down in an air battle and, severely wounded, attempted a forced landing at Great Dixter, Northiam. In doing so, his 222 Squadron Spitfire over

7-8. (Below & top right) Limping home from a raid on Croydon aerodrome, this Messerschmitt 110 put down at School Farm, Hooe, on 15th August 1940, where the two crew were captured - the gunner seriously wounded. Later, the aeroplane was covered over with camouflage to avoid detection and attack from other German aeroplanes who would have attempted to destroy this captured "prize".

turned, but Edridge was dragged clear and taken to the nearby Military Hospital which had been set up in Brickwall House. Here, some hours later, Edridge succumbed to his wounds, but his plight so affected the civilian ambulance driver who had rescued him that he wrote a moving letter of condolence to Edridge's parents. Such actions were typical of Britain's civilian population, thrown very much into the thick of the conflict as history was being made and their liberty won around them.

9. When Unteroffizier Kaiser landed his crippled Messerschmitt 109 at Broomhill Farm, Camber, on 24th August 1940, the aircraft struck poles which had been erected as an anti-invasion measure against glider landings. As it slewed round the aeroplane broke in half and caught fire, although Kaiser escaped with his life.

10. All that was left when Oblt. Josef Volk baled out of his Messerschmitt 109 north of Rye was this smoking crater at Blackwall Bridge, on 11th November 1940.

11. Sgt. Pilot Whipps sits astride his Spitfire of 602 Squadron at Westhampnett (now Goodwood) aerodrome. On 6th September 1940, Whipps was shot down over Peasmarsh, but survived as he took to his parachute. Sadly, George Whipps was killed in a flying accident on 26th August 1941.

12. This Messerschmitt 109 plunged 30ft into the soft soil at Lower Lidham Hill Farm, Guestling, on 25th October 1940, after Willi Koslowski had been forced to abandon his burning aeroplane.   The wreckage remained entombed and perfectly preserved until September 1989, when it was salvaged by a team from the Tangmere Military Aviation Museum.

13. Pilot Officer Hilary Edridge, a 21 year old Spitfire pilot of 222 Squadron, attempted to make an emergency landing after being wounded in an air battle over Northiam on 30th October 1940.   Lifting his aircraft clear of Great Dixter House, he crashed in one of the fields beyond and overturned.   Dragged clear, he died of his wounds later that day in Brickwall Hospital, Northiam.

Edridge Close, in Elm Park, Hornchurch was named in his memory.

14. In common with many large country houses, Brickwall at Northiam was commandeered for military use, in this instance becoming an emergency hospital.

The Orchard
Northiam
E. Sussex.

Oct 31st '40.

Dear Mr Colridge I felt you would like to have some direct news of your Son, from somebody who actually saw - was with him after his crash. I am the Ambulance Driver who went to him - took him to Brickwall Hospital, a want to assure you that everything possible was done for his comfort. I myself held blankets to screen him from the wind, while the First Aid Party were dressing his wounds. He crashed about 11.30 A.M., was found at once, cut out of his parachute - his wound dressed a then taken to Hospital. He passed on about 1.30 p.m., but I know he was unconscious all the time & knew nothing of what had happened, I am sure. The reason, I think of his crash, was, a bullet wound in the head - If there is anything you would like to ask me please don't hesitate. I shall be only to happy to help & answer anything.

Yrs Sincerely
Betty Rogers

20

BEXHILL MUNICIPAL BOROUGH

Almost before the Battle of Britain had got underway, a Junkers Ju88 bomber circled the town early on the morning of 28th July 1940, and was then seen in a shallow descent beyond Sidley. Eventually the bomber slid to a halt in a clover field at Buckholt Farm, Watermill Lane, almost undamaged save for bent propellers The four crew clambered out unhurt and when the authorities arrived to take them into custody they were found sipping tea in the kitchen of Buckholt Farmhouse! Later the aeroplane was carefully dismantled, reassembled and test flown by the RAF.

After this exciting start to the wartime life of Bexhill, it was inevitable that the reality of armed conflict would soon strike. August 21st saw the first bombs, which fell harmlessly on open ground near Lower Barnhorn Farm and from this date onwards there were almost daily occurrences of bombing, machine gunning and aerial battles. Bombs hit the town in a bad way

on 26th September when thirty five high explosive devices were dropped. In this raid, the Bexhill Stationmaster, Mr.P.T.Perkins, had a remarkable escape. As he threw himself to the ground on the platform at Central Station, two bombs burst each side of him. Not so lucky was Mr.W.G.Reeves proprietor of a newsagents in Town Hall Square who was one of the casualties as twenty bombs straddled the town.

Bombings with all the attendant death and destruction continued to be a way of life in Bexhill for the remainder of the war. Primarily, very much a civilian town with little in the way of legitimate military targets Bexhill did, however, house an Initial Training Wing for prospective aircrew candidates of the RAF. Later, many of these young men who were to be seen marching through the town would be in action in the skies above this very coastline.

15. This motley uniformed searchlight crew posed alongside the Junkers 88 which ran out of fuel and made a forced landing in a field at Buckholt Farm off Watermill Lane, Sidley, on 28th July 1940.

16. Emblazoned beneath the cockpit was the colourful "edelweiss" emblem of Luftwaffe bomber group KG.51. This is the other side of the aircraft seen in the previous picture.

17. Dismantled and re-assembled the same aircraft is pictured here under repair at Farnborough. Later it was repainted in British markings and test flown by the RAF.

BOGNOR REGIS URBAN DISTRICT

With its close proximity to the aerodromes at Ford and Tangmere, it was inevitable that Bognor should see its fair share of action and, although no enemy aircraft were actually brought down on land during 1940 within the boundaries of Bognor itself, a number were observed falling into the sea offshore. However, they were not only machines of the enemy, for on 26th August Sgt. Cyril Babbage of the Westhampnett based 602 Squadron was obliged to bale out of his shot-up Spitfire off Bognor following an intense air battle. Babbage was rescued from the sea by rowing boat and brought ashore on the beach none the worse for his experience. Later on during the battle a fellow pilot of Babbage's, Sgt. Elcombe of the same squadron, made a forced landing in his Spitfire on Felpham Golf Course and walked away unharmed. Not so fortunate was Uffz.Rudolf Miese, shot out of the sky above Bognor on 15th November by a Spitfire flown by Sgt. Glendinning of 74 Squadron. As the flaming wreckage of his Messerschmitt 109 fell into the sea just below the waters edge, a badly burned Miese parachuted into the town and five years captivity!

18-19. Lucky to be alive, Sgt. Pilot Cyril Babbage of 602 Squadron was rescued from the sea off Bognor by rowing boat after baling out of his Spitfire during a dog-fight on 26th August 1940. Unsure of his nationality, his rescuers took two armed soldiers with them - just in case!

20-21. Quite a reception committee awaited Cyril Babbage as he waded ashore with a welcome cigarette being lit for him by a policeman. In the background is Bognor Pier, with its dismantled centre section which had been removed to prevent its use as an enemy landing stage.

24

BRIGHTON COUNTY BOROUGH

With anticipation of imminent invasion, Brighton found itself amidst the Ministry of Home Security's "banned" South Coast area which, in Sussex, stretched from Rye to Littlehampton. Access to and from these areas was strictly controlled with police and military road blocks and a dusk-to-dawn curfew for those living inside an area roughly 300 yards north of Brighton seafront. The front itself was unrecognisable from its pre-war gaiety. Gone were the amusements, deck chairs and ice cream vendors. Armed troops walked the promenades where holiday makers had strolled the year before. The beaches were deserted and mined, and barbed wire coils stretched the length of the seafront.

Both piers had sections blown out of their centres to deny usage as enemy landing stages, whilst the hotels were deserted, or else requisitioned for military occupation and sandbagged. The story at Brighton was, of course, repeated at all of the seaside towns. Again, like most of the Sussex seaside towns, Brighton was hit heavily by the bombers, but undoubtedly the most tragic incident was on Saturday 14th September, when a single bomb scored a direct hit on the Odeon Cinema, Kemp Town, during a matinee performance attended mostly by children. A total of 59 people died as the bomb exploded in the auditorium.

Inevitably, the effect of war upon industry and commerce was to divert just about every available resource towards the war effort, with food production geared up for survival and self-sufficiency whilst factories turned much of their output over to war materials. Transport, too, was a valuable resource and the Brighton transport and haulage company, A.V. Nicholls & Co., was engaged by the Air Ministry to provide vehicles and men to collect the wreckages of British and German aircraft from across Southern England and convey them to a large dump at 49 Maintenance Unit, RAF Faygate, near Horsham. (See also Horsham Rural District). Throughout the battle, A.V.Nicholls removed scores of wrecked aircraft from around Kent and Sussex, the employees soon becoming skilled and adept at dismantling and removing aircraft!

During the Battle of Britain itself, no aircraft actually fell within the confines of the Borough, although excitement was caused during May 1940 when a Dutch Air Force Fokker seaplane landed off Brighton Beach and was pulled up onto the foreshore. On board were the Dutch Foreign Minister, Dr. Van der Kleffens, his wife and M. Welter, Dutch Minister for the Colonies, who had made good their escape as Holland fell to the Germans. Later, and as the battle itself drew to a conclusion, a Messerschmitt 109 was shot down into the sea off the Palace Pier on 17th November with the loss of its pilot. Later, on 21st of that month, the channel claimed another aircraft and its crew as a Beaufighter of 219 Squadron flew into the sea off Brighton.

22. There was drama off Brighton seafront on 10th January 1940, when a Fleet Air Arm Hawker Nimrod on a coastal reconnaissance crashed into the sea about ½ mile off the beach. The aeroplane, number K4627, was towed ashore by fishing boats and its pilot, the only occupant, was rescued from the water.

23. Although pictured in 1941, Arthur Nicholls the Brighton haulage contractor is seen here (centre, wearing the Homburg hat) with a Junkers 88 arriving for exhibition outside the Corn Exchange, Brighton, for a War Weapons Exhibition. Arthur Nicholl's haulage company was contracted by the Air Ministry during 1940 to recover the wrecks of shot down aircraft throughout Sussex.

BURGESS HILL URBAN DISTRICT

Legend has it that "Lord Haw-Haw" frequently referred to the bombing of Burgess Hill Aerodrome in his broadcasts from Germany. However, no such aerodrome of course existed and it must be assumed that any such reference related to Biggin Hill aerodrome in Kent, and not Sussex! All the same, one of the first close encounters with the Luftwaffe came on 18th August as Dornier 17's roared low over the town en-route from Kenley, but it was not until October that the bombings really started for Burgess Hill. On the 14th a bomb fell in the garden of Captain Wormald at Mill Road but failed to explode, causing local disruption until it could be defused some days later. On the 16th, four high explosive and one oil bomb dropped, but this time all of them exploded. Damage was caused to the back of the police station with other damage caused to Park Road and Crescent Road. In Park Road gas and water mains were damaged. Four days later on the 20th yet more bombs were to fall, this time two high explosives damaged "Blenheims" in Keymer Road.

24. This is how the Luftwaffe saw Royal George Road, Burgess Hill, as they roared low over the rooftops en-route to bomb RAF Kenley at lunchtime on Sunday, 18th August 1940. Taken from the cockpit, the spinner cone of the port propeller can be seen on the left of the photograph.

CHAILEY RURAL DISTRICT

Despite the size of this geographical area, there were only two fatal civilian casualties sustained in the region throughout 1940; forty year old Gwendolyn Lindop dying in an incident at St. Ann Without on 13th October and eighty year old Gilbert Harriott dying from shock when a bomb fell near Riddens Cottages, Plumpton, on 22nd December.

One of the first aircraft losses in the area was the crash of a Hurricane of 601 Squadron at Southease on 4th July 1940, when Sgt. Jensen was lucky to escape with his life as his aircraft overturned in an emergency landing following engine failure over the sea. Nevertheless, he was seriously injured and spent some months in hospital before returning to flying duties. Just over one month later, on 18th August, a group of low flying Dornier 17's swept over Southease en-route for RAF Kenley and, as they passed, snapped a remarkably clear photograph of the railway line at Southease Halt with the cement works beyond.

On 1st October, a Messerschmitt 109 was shot down over Falmer and went into a screaming power dive with its young pilot, Hans Bluder, slumped dead over his controls. The 400mph plus impact within the South Down chalk at Balmer Farm blew the fighter to smithereens. No trace of Bluder was ever found. On the 12th, at Iford Farm, Sgt. Cyril Babbage of the Westhampnett based 602 Squadron made an emergency wheels-down landing and, as he over-ran his landing field, the undercarriage caught in a hedgerow and flipped the Spitfire over onto its back. Miraculously, Babbage escaped unharmed

25. **Unlucky thirteen! Uffz. Raisinger escaped unharmed when he belly landed his shot up Messerschmitt 109 at Harvey Cross near Saltdean on 25th October 1940.**

having led a charmed life since his earlier rescue from the sea off Bognor on 26th August! Also, within the parish of Iford, at Harveys Cross Farm, Gefr.Karl Raisinger had a lucky escape of sorts as his shot-up Messerschmitt slithered to a halt on the downland. To Raisinger, though, the number "13" emblazoned on the fuselage must have spelt bad luck as he was marched off to captivity! Not so fortunate were three crew members of a Dornier 17, shot down at South Heighton and who were lost as their aircraft exploded on impact. Only one of their number,

Uffz.G.Weinhold, managed to make good an escape and descended by parachute. Rounding off the year, a 253 Squadron Hurricane put down at Falmer on 1st December with a wounded Polish Pilot, Sgt.Szymon Kita, on board. Later, one of his rescuers, Police Superintendent Britton, visited him in hospital taking along a rare wartime treat of oranges. Here, the grateful Kita muttered in broken English "Jerry very strong". Fortunately, this Polish hero of Churchill's Few survived the Battle of Britain and, indeed, the entire war.

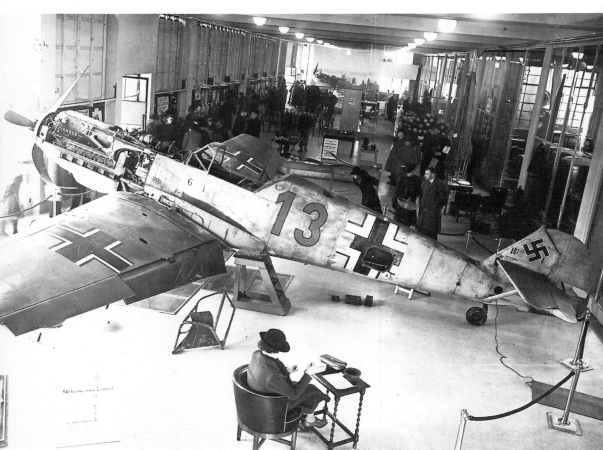

26. Seen in the previous picture, Karl Raisinger's aeroplane was to be put to use raising pennies for the "Spitfire Fund" when it was exhibited at Messrs. Rootes car showrooms in Maidstone. Sixpence was the price for a peep into the cockpit. That's a mere 200,000 inquisitive stares to pay for a Spitfire!

27. Taken minutes before the picture of Burgess Hill, the same photographer snapped this shot of the railway line and halt at Southease from the other side of his Dornier 17 cockpit. Again, the propeller spinner cone can be seen on the right. In the distance is the Cement Works.

28. Sgt. Cyril Babbage (once again!!) escaped unharmed as his Spitfire trundled through a hedge (note the two holes made by the passage of the undercarriage), dug its propeller into the ground and flipped over.

29. Somewhere in the fields shown in picture 27, Sgt. Pilot Jensen of 601 Squadron had a lucky escape when his Hurricane overturned in an emergency landing following engine failure on 4th July 1940. Here, his aeroplane is seen later at a civilian repair depot.

30. Soldiers gather the scattered debris of Hans Bluder's Messerschmitt 109 strewn across farmland at Balmer Farm, Falmer, on 1st October 1940, after it had been shot down by Pilot Officer George Bennions in a Spitfire of 41 Squadron. No trace of Bluder was ever found.

CHANCTONBURY RURAL DISTRICT

Although covering just about one-sixth of the entire geographical region of West Sussex, there was minimal civilian loss of life as the result of enemy action during 1940, despite hectic aerial activity throughout that period.

First enemy losses in the district occurred on 16th August, when a Messerschmitt 110 was forced down in a cornfield at Lee Farm, Rackham, and its two crew captured whilst at Annington Farm, Bramber, a Heinkel HeIII came down. In this incident, three of the crew were captured, but two had been killed in the fighter attack prior to landing. September 4th again saw fierce action in the district with Messerschmitt 110's being shot down at Washington, Pulborough and Steyning. The aircraft down at Washington plunged

vertically into a field at Church Farm, leaving no trace of aeroplane or occupants above ground, although the exact position has since been covered over by a new dual-carriageway by-pass. Five days later, Oberleutnlant Erwin Daig had a luckier escape when he force landed his Messerschmitt 109 at Charity Farm, Storrington, and was taken POW. More dramatic, however, was the loss of a Junkers Ju88 at Storrington. Attempting to return home from Birmingham where it had been hit by "flak", the pilot tried to make a forced landing and thus save his crew. Approaching Storrington, the aircraft released its remaining bomb load, with six or seven bombs falling from West Chiltington Golf Course, across Hurston Place, down Hurston Lane and

31. As they prepare to dismantle it, a salvage party pose cheerfully with the Heinkel 111 at Anningtons Farm, Bramber, shot down there on 16th August 1940.

straddling the A283 where one failed to explode and another detonated in a field behind No. 41 Main Street, Storrington. The explosion shattered windows, damaged the roof and brought down ceilings at No. 41, the residence of Mr and Mrs Waller. Their three year old son had a lucky escape, being safely tucked up in the shelter beneath the stairs, his cot in the room above being crushed by the collapsing ceiling. The stricken Junkers finally struck the ground at "Greyfriars", Waterworks Lane, but broke up on hitting trees; the crash taking the lives of two of the crew, whilst another, badly injured, died the next day. Meanwhile, Ron Lampton, who lived at West Lodge, "Greyfriars", was away in Wiltshire serving in the Army and was surprised to pick up the newspapers on Sunday 3rd November, and recognise pictures of his house and garden with the wreckage of a bomber strewn all around it!

These, then, were the losses sustained by the Luftwaffe over Chanctonbury Rural District, but the RAF, too, suffered its own casualties. First down was Sgt.Jim Hallowes of Tangmere's 43 Sqn, forced to make an emergency landing beside the River Arun at Amberley, and on 1st October a Spitfire was lost in an air battle over Henfield. Having just despatched the Messerschmitt 109 of Hans Bluder at Falmer, (see Chailey RD) Pilot Officer George Bennions of 41 Squadron was hit by cannon fire and seriously wounded. One of the cannon shells exploded on the cockpit canopy, blinding him in one eye and causing serious wounds to his head and face. Almost unconscious, George Bennions floated down on his parachute at Dunstalls Farm and his life was saved by prompt treatment at Horsham Hospital and later at East Grinstead. His Spitfire crashed beside the road at Heatenthorn Farm and in 1974, George Bennions attended the exhumation of wreckage from his old aeroplane. The landowner, so impressed by the story of George Bennions' courage, named one of his racehorses in his honour, "Bennions Spitfire".

George Bennions was the only serious RAF casualty in the district throughout the Battle of Britain and, as mentioned previously, very few civilians were killed or injured in the region during this period. One, however, deserves a mention for, on 4th October, Air Raid Warden The Revd William Masefield died whilst cycling on the Stopham Road at Pulborough. German bombs and gunfire were no respecters of age, sex, or status. Today, a roadside plaque marks the spot where this servant of the community lost his life.

32. This Junkers 88 had been targetted to Birmingham when it was hit by "Ack Ack" fire and forced down at "Greyfriars", Storrington, on the night of 1st November 1940. Soldiers and airmen examine the badly broken up aeroplane - no doubt hunting for souvenirs!

33. PC Harry Birch amidst the corn stooks at Lee Farm, Clapham, on 16th August 1940, guards the Messerschmitt 110, which can just be made out above his head, while the faint line above the stooks to the left is a skid mark made by the landing aeroplane.

34. Deep in thought and perhaps pondering on what might have been, George Bennions (left) examines the salvaged propeller of the Spitfire he left behind in a hurry on 1st October 1940 when he re-visits the scene in 1974

35. At approximately 0740 hours on 20th July 1940, the engine of this 43 Squadron Hurricane siezed up solid after the loss of all oil pressure. The pilot, Sgt. Jim Hallowes, made a very skilful wheels-up landing in a field at Amberley, tearing off the tail wheel on the anti-glider posts around the field. There are grounds for believing that the oil tank had not been checked prior to flight in spite of a signature in the aeroplane log book. Later, it became known that a certain ground crew Flight Sergeant went out to the crash and surreptitiously poured in four gallons of used oil, all the while proclaiming in a loud voice for the benefit of the Army guard "This will stop the engine corroding until they come to pick it up!"

CHICHESTER MUNICIPAL BOROUGH

As the main town in the district it was natural that the city should attract servicemen in their hundreds to relax during their off-duty hours, the city's pubs being favourite haunts of soldiers, sailors and airmen. In particular, high spirited parties by groups of airmen and pilots from the nearby aerodromes became regular events, but, by day, these same men earned the respect of Chichester's residents who witnessed their aerial exploits in combat with the Luftwaffe. Indeed, one of the most spectacular incidents of the Battle of Britain took place on 18th August, when a Junkers Ju87 "Stuka" dive-bomber was caught by RAF fighters and sent into a near vertical howling dive above the rooftops of Chichester. Its headlong passage was caught on film by a photographer standing somewhere near the old bus station, and this now famous picture was later seen around the world in newspapers and magazines. When it hit the ground near Whitehouse Farm, the force of impact drove the engine and bomb deep into the ground. Today, a post war housing estate off The Broyle has covered any trace of the buried wreckage and, quite probably, a 250Kg bomb.

Despite its city status and occasional bombings and machine gunning incidents, there were few fatal casualties in the borough during 1940, although the Civilian War Dead Register could give a false impression that this was not the case, as many casualties brought into St. Richards Hospital from outlying regions subsequently died there later. There were, of course, many many others who owed their lives to the splendid work carried out here on injured civilians and RAF pilots. Even Luftwaffe airmen sometimes had the medical and nursing staff of St. Richards to thank for their survival.

36. Oblt. Wilhelm, pilot of a Junkers 87 Stuka shot down into Fishbourne Creek on 18th August 1940, is marched off into captivity with an Army escort at Chichester Railway Station. Next stop would have been London and the POW interrogation centre at Cockfosters and then incarceration in a camp. For Johannes Wilhelm the war was over!

37. Roaring down above the rooftops of Chichester, this Junkers 87 smashed into the ground at Whitehouse Farm off the Broyle. One can almost hear the howl and roar as this dive bomber makes its terminal dive!

38. Aftermath! All that remained when the Stuka hit the ground was unrecognisable twisted and charred metal. Little of any value here for the souvenir hunters - and even less for RAF Intelligence.

CHICHESTER RURAL DISTRICT

With its proximity to military targets and airfields, it was inevitable that the district would see its fair share of air fighting. Indeed, as a direct result, no fewer than twenty three enemy aircraft came down in the area during 1940. Surprisingly, despite this cost to the Luftwaffe, there were comparatively few deaths in the area, but on 19th August there were at least three civilian fatalities at Broadreads Holiday Camp, Selsey, caused by a bombing on this day. It is believed those killed were evacuees from the capital, one being thirteen year old Thomas Martin of Poplar, London.

First loss to the Luftwaffe was sustained when a Heinkel HeIII was shot down in flames onto East Beach, Selsey, on 11th July by Hurricanes of 145 Squadron from Westhampnett. Two of the crew perished, but the other three were taken as POWs. Just over a week later, on the 21st, a Messerschmitt 110 was forced down almost intact on to Home Farm, Goodwood, its two crew captured.

Such was the condition of their aeroplane that it was dismantled, repaired and subsequently test flown by the RAF.

Throughout August there continued an almost regular rain of German hardware on to the region, but it was on the 16th of that month that war came to the rural district with a vengeance. No fewer than five German machines and two British planes were scattered across the surrounding countryside whilst part of Tangmere airfield lay in smoking ruins. On the airfield itself, at the height of a pounding dive-bombing attack by "Stukas", a crippled Hurricane landed in flames, its pilot seriously injured. Pilot Officer "Billy" Fiske, an American volunteer, had made it back to the base of his 601 Squadron, although he subsequently died in hospital of his injuries, becoming the first US citizen to die on active service in England. Laid to rest in the churchyard at Boxgrove Priory, Fiske was later honoured by a plaque in the crypt of St. Paul's Cathedral commemorating how this young

39. Two Gloster Gladiator bi-planes of 605 Squadron collided in mid air near Tangmere on 19th September 1939. The pilot of one, Fg. Off. Warren, was killed whilst the second officer, Fg. Off. Forbes, baled out safely. This was the wreckage of one of the aeroplanes but the exact location is not recorded. The farm buildings on the skyline should provide a point of reference. Perhaps a reader will be able to identify the spot?

man had died for Britain.

Just down the road from Tangmere, at Shopwhyke House, a Messerschmitt 110 was brought down by Fiske's CO later that day. It was almost an act of revenge for Billy and for the havoc caused earlier in the bombing as Squadron Leader Sir Archibald Hope, Bt, sent the Messerschmitt roaring vertically into a pond in the grounds, and in full view of the entire squadron, pilots and ground crew. No doubt a morale boosting tonic for all!

Two days later, on the 18th, the eerie roar and howl of the Stukas returned to the district, but this time seeking different targets. Thorney Island, Poling and Ford were all hit badly, but once again at a price to Goerings much vaunted Stukas. At Cut Mill in West Ashling, North Barn at Chidham, and in Fishbourne Creek the smashed wreckages of Junkers 87s could be found, whilst offshore the Channel claimed yet more victims. Oberleutnant Johannes Wilhelm and his gunner, Anton Worner, were forced to bale out of their Stuka before they had a chance to deliver their bombs on Thorney Island, leaving the bomber to plop into the glutinous mud of Fishbourne Creek from where it and its deadly bomb load were retrieved in recent years.

The following day saw a marked reduction in aerial activity, but Pilot Officer Henry Moody of 602 Squadron had to bale out of his Spitfire, having been hit by defensive fire from a Junkers Ju88. Despite burns to his hands, Moody survived as his aeroplane crashed into a ditch on Colworth Farm near Merston.

The 26th August again saw heavy fighting with a Heinkel HeIII shot down onto the sands at Bracklesham Bay, West Wittering. Of five crew members all but the pilot had been shot dead and the events which followed have since lead to speculation and rumour that the four airmen were shot dead in cold blood by British soldiers, the sensational press of the 1970s carrying stories with such headlines as "Was This our Secret War Crime?". The truth has since been confirmed by Alfred Metger, the surviving pilot, who tells how that, one by one, his comrades were shot dead around him in the air battle. Nevertheless, the folklore lives on in the area and no doubt fuelled by the more recent press interest in the event, an interest which waned when the less dramatic truth was uncovered! The Heinkel, though, was covered up intact, as it sank beneath the sands sucked down by the passage of time and tides.

Less intact was the Heinkel HeIII which, hit by ground fire, smashed itself to pieces amongst the beech trees on the estate of Stansted House, Stoughton, whilst on a low-level bombing mission. As the bomb load exploded, it took the lives of all five crew and mortally wounded an RAF Pilot Officer, Gilbert Elliot, as he ran from Stanstead House where he was billeted. Picking over the wreckage, the only point of interest which RAF Intelligence Officers could find worthy of note was a section of tailfin, marked with a yellow shield and bearing three red fishes.

On the 29th of that month there was a tragedy for Tangmere based 213 Squadron when one of their Hurricanes was shot down into the sea off Selsey Bill. Pilot Officer Richard Hutley was plucked from the sea by the Selsey Lifeboat "Canadian Pacific" but, unfortunately, all efforts by the crew to revive him failed. A rare arrival for this part of Sussex was a Messerschmitt 109, shot down almost intact by a Belgian Pilot, P/O Jean Offenberg of 145 Squadron, at Mapsons Farm, Sidlesham. The pilot was captured, although it will be noted that comparatively few examples of this aeroplane came down in West Sussex. Restrictions on its operational range, through fuel limitations, made operations this far a hazardous business, with little or no available "combat time" for those who made it this far west.

With the air war now shifting primarily from daytime to nighttime activities the meagre night fighter defences of the RAF were being strengthened, with any victories over enemy bombers a great boost to morale. Such was the case when a Junkers Ju88 exploded into the ground at Stocks Lane, East Wittering, on the night of 20th November. The plane had fallen victim to Flight Lt. John Cunningham in a radar equipped Beaufighter of 504 Squadron and, as it went into its terminal dive, three of the crew baled out. One of them, Heinrich Liebermann, was left behind, shot dead as he lay at his bomb sight. Two of the remaining three survived, but the third, Peter May, drifted down in the darkness to land in the icy waters of the Channel where, sadly, he was to perish. Apart from a few crumpled sections of wing and the tailwheel strewn around a deep water filled pit of wreckage, nothing much

40. Firemen, soldiers, an RAF airman and a Local Defence Volunteer armed with a double barelled shotgun examine the fragmentary remains of the Junkers 87 Stuka shot down at North Barn, Chidham, on 18th August 1940. Little did they realise thart buried beneath their feet was an unexploded 250 Kg Bomb! This was subsequently found in the 1970s when the site was excavated.

41. Groundcrew of 145 Squadron pose at Westhampnett with a trophy retrieved from the Heinkel 111 shot down by the Squadron onto East Beach, Selsey, on 11th July 1940. In the background can be seen one of the Squadron Hurricanes.

remained of the aeroplane. Today, nothing marks the spot which has been covered over by the turf of a post-war playing field. In spite of the scale of aerial warfare across most of Sussex, the passage of time has meant that nature has erased most of the scars, or else notable buildings, sites or landmarks of events in 1940 vanished before the developers bulldozers. More durable, though, are the memories - and sometimes the scars-left in the minds of those who were there. The civilians of Chichester Rural District were certainly there in the thick of it, and some paid the price. Sixty four year old Henry Ayling of Westgate, Chichester, was one such casualty; he was caught as the Stukas hit Tangmere on 16th August. He became just one of many civilian fatalities in the region during the Battle.

42. Typical of Squadron emblems applied to German aircraft this Junkers 88 shot down at Mudberry Farm, Bosham, on 21st September 1940, sports the red griffon on a white shield of LG.1.

→
43. The railway line can be made out in the background, as two soldiers examine one of the propeller assemblies torn from the bomber in the crash landing.

→
44. This Messerschmitt 110 was forced down on Home Farm, Goodwood, in July 1940 by three Hurricanes. Earlier, it is thought that this aeroplane was responsible for shooting down an unarmed bi-plane trainer over Wiltshire, killing the naval rating pilot. Seen here, partly dismantled by No. 5 Party, 49 Maintenance Unit, the aeroplane was later to test fly in the hands of the RAF.

45. A Tangmere based Hurricane of No. 1 Squadron taxies past a parked 615 Squadron Gladiator at Ford during September 1939. Within days, No. 1 Squadron was sent to France and was soon in the thick of the fighting. Ford aerodrome was badly hit by a dive bombing attack afrom Junkers 87 "Stuka's" on 18th August 1940.

46-47. Just a water filled pit and scattered wreckage is all that remains of the Junkers 88 shot down by Flt. Lt. John "Cats Eyes" Cunningham on 28th November 1940. Judging from these photographs there was more here to interest the local schoolboy population than RAF Intelligence Officer Flt. Lt. Michael Golovine as he studies a crumpled wing section at Stubcroft Farm, Stocks Lane, West Wittering.

48-49. As a soldier points out the bullet-holed nose of this Junkers 88 in Pagham Harbour on 9th September 1940, his colleagues indulge in a spot of souvenir hunting and remove the swastika from its tail. The swooping eagle emblem indicates the unit to be KG.30 and one of those on board was a Major Hackbarth, son-in-law of General Field Marshall Kesselring. Hackbarth was seriously wounded, another crewman died whilst the other two became prisoners of war.

→
50. Soon to be engulfed by the tide and sucked into the sands, this Heinkel 111 was shot down at Bracklesham Bay Beach on 26th August 1940. Some of the crew were buried in Chichester Cemetery; their deaths later causing some speculation that they had been shot in cold blood by their captors - a rumour subsequently disproved!

51-52. There seems little point in guarding the meagre remnants of this Heinkel 111 which blew up at Stanstead Park, Stoughton, on 8th October 1940, but a Home Guardsman does his duty all the same! Intelligence Officers noted that a yellow shield bearing three red fishes was painted on the tail. This emblem is seen on another aircraft of the same unit, 8/KG.55. In fact, 2808 was a sister aircraft of the one lost at Stoughton which was 2809.

53. More unusual than the average road traffic accident, this Junkers 87 Stuka has veered off the B2145 Selsey Road, left its undercarriage beind on the grass verge and ended up in a field after being hit by RAF fighters on 16th August 1940. Both occupants survived, although one was seriously wounded. The exact location is on the west side of the road, just south of the junction to Church Norton.

54. Another battered Stuka which was lost after the Tangmere raid on 16th August. This one flew through trees at Bowley Farm, South Mundham before rolling to a halt in this condition with its pilot and gunner both dead. Once again, it proves to be a popular attraction for the locals!

55.   This ornamental pond was enlarged by the
Messerschmitt 110 which plunged into it at Shopwyke
House, near Tangmere, on 16th August 1940, becoming
the grave for aeroplane and crew.   Not much remained
above ground as this gardener contemplates the
clean-up.

CUCKFIELD RURAL DISTRICT

First casualty in the region was Sgt. Pilot Spencer of 79 Squadron, Biggin Hill, who crashed as the result of a flying accident at Three Bridges on 26th April 1940, but another four months were to pass before aerial activity resulted in the loss of any further aircraft in the district. On 30th August, a Heinkel HeIII bomber was shot down by fighters at Ashfold Crossways, Lower Beeding, exploding and scattering wreckage far and wide, killing two of its crew whilst the other three had managed to bale out safely.

September 9th saw particularly heavy air fighting over the district and out of the fray a Junkers Ju88 was seen to descend under control but obviously damaged above the parish of Barcombe, eventually landing in a field at Court House Farm. The drama that subsequently unfolded has gone down in local folklore, and tells how that one of the crew (allegedly a member of the Gestapo!) was shot dead by other crew members after the forced landing following an argument amongst the crew. The truth, however, was less dramatic. Hit by fighters over London, one of the crew members, Ernst Diebler, was shot dead and with the aircraft disabled, Barcombe was the furthest point the aircraft managed to reach as it struggled to head home. After landing the three unharmed crewmen gently lifted their dead comrade from the wreck and carried his body to safety before setting fire to their near intact Junkers Ju88. Those observing from a distance heard shouts from the crew, and then a loud report as the demolition charge exploded and incinerated the aircraft. These actions, and the fact that Diebler's body was found some distance away from the plane doubtless led to the rumour mongering - so rife during wartime - which subsequently established the folk-lore and legend as historical fact! No legend, however, surrounds the loss of a Messerschmitt 109 shot down into the pond at Cinderhill Farm, Horsted Keynes. The facts were quite straightforward and brutally blunt when described in official reports, telling how the fighter dived into the pond and all but vanished from sight. Alfred Sander, its pilot, went with his aeroplane into the water and mire, but today the pond is filled

in and grassed over. Nothing remains to show what happened here fifty years ago. A week later, on 8th October, a Junkers 88 crashed and disintegrated across farmland at Toovies Farm, Worth, snuffing out the lives of its four crew. Sadly, a farmworker who was nearby on his tractor was sprayed with blazing aviation spirit and died later from his injuries.

Most of the aircraft lost in the district fell from the sky as the result of combat, but on the night of 30th October, a Beaufighter of 219 Squadron flew into trees at Balcombe Place, its two crew the victims of a tragic accident.

With the Battle of Britain over, the night blitz and its heavy bombing began. Two victims in Cuckfield Rural District were Harold Attwater and Leonard Bargus who died as they worked on the Southern Railway between Balcombe and Three Bridges on 9th December.

56. Yet another of the remarkable series of pictures snapped from one of the Dorner 17s as they overflew Sussex en-route to bomb Kenley on 18th Augusut 1940. This view is of Cyprus Road, Burgess Hill, at 1.09pm, taken as people dash for cover. The light coloured sand-bagged building was in use as an Air Raid Warden's post whilst the "tram-lines" on the road were, in fact, four strips of newly laid road surfacing.

57-58 Oily black smoke stains the sky at Barcombe as the Junkers 88 incinerates itself at Court Lodge Farm, Barcombe, having been fired by its crew on landing. Oblt. Hans Gollnish was the captain of the aircraft.

CUCKFIELD URBAN DISTRICT

Comprising Haywards Heath, Cuckfield and Lindfield the district saw widespread bombing, but no fatalities. Nevertheless, damage was considerable when bombs fell during the evening of 28th September in a garden of a house at Haywards Road, Haywards Heath. Damage was also caused to property in Wood Ride, Park Road, South Road, Ashenground Road and Sussex Road. Although the daylight air raids and dog fights had all but ceased by December, the 6th saw a bomb falling in Brook Street, Cuckfield, blasting a huge crater and causing much damage but a bomb which fell in Cuckfield on the 21st demolished a house in Hanlye Lane, trapping its occupants. Both managed to crawl out of the debris and walked to the hospital nearby before help had arrived!

Whilst no aeroplane fell within the administrative district a sad ceremony was performed on Thursday 26th September at Haywards Heath Cemetery. Here, in the presence of many townsfolk and locals, Flying Officer Richard Plummer was laid to rest. Richard was well known in the locality, being the son of Mr George Plummer, Surveyor to the Cuckfield Urban District Council. He had died following wounds received in an air battle over Essex on 4th September whilst piloting a Hurricane of 46 Squadron.

59. Local hero. Fg. Off. Richard Plummer, a fighter pilot with 46 Squadron, was wounded over Essex on 4th September 1940 and died of his wounds ten days later. A local boy, he was buried in Haywards Heath Cemetery, his home town.

EASTBOURNE COUNTY BOROUGH

Eastbourne, which holds the dubious claim to fame of being the most raided town in the South East, was certainly the first in Sussex to witness at first hand the grim reality of war. On 20th March 1940, the British merchant ship SS Barn Hill was bombed off Beachy Head whilst en-route from Halifax to London with general cargo. A number of the crew were killed in the attack which set fire to the ship and disabled her. Gallant rescue work was carried out by the Eastbourne lifeboat "Jane Holland", two of who's crew earned RNLI bravery awards, with Bronze Medals going to life-boatmen Huggett and Allchorn and a framed letter of appreciation to Coxswain Hardy. Later, the Barn Hill was beached at Langney Point where thousands of tins of canned food spilled into the sea and onto the beaches, providing a rich but illicit harvest with which the townsfolk of Eastbourne supplemented their meagre wartime rations for many months!

Tragedy and heroism again went hand-in-hand at Eastbourne when, on 28th September, a number of bombs were dropped across the town causing widespread devastation. Damage was particularly severe in the Cavendish Place area where one bomb demolished Nos. 69-71. Here, rescuers toiled for thirty six hours to reach trapped victims one of whom, seventeen year old Peggy Harland, was trapped by her legs but conscious and cheerful throughout much of her ordeal. As they worked to free her, a delayed action bomb lay nearby. Eventually, an emergency operation was carried out to amputate Peggy's legs but, sadly, she died in hospital on 30th September. Peggy, a Girl Guide, was posthumously awarded the Girl Guides Gilt Cross for gallantry. Her rescuers, too, were honoured. George Medals were awarded to A.E.Blackmer, E.L.Turner, E.H.May and F.C.F.Stevens with an MBE to Chief Officer S.A.Phillips of the Eastbourne Fire Brigade.

Without doubt, the most alarming incident of the period occurred on 16th August, when a Messerschmitt 110 was shot down over Meads. The disintegrating fighter hurtled out of the clouds in a crescendo of sound with both engines screaming at full throttle before

60. Ablaze off Eastbourne, the S.S. Barn-Hill is attended by a tug from Newhaven (Foremost) and Eastbourne Lifeboat (Jane Holland) as she drifts on 21st March 1940, after being bombed the night before.

61. Later, beached at Langney Point, scores of people flock onto the beaches to salvage some of the spilled cargo. Tinned food and cheeses provided rich pickings, and despite warnings against this illicit pillaging the looting continued unabated for days!

62. Civilian First Aid parties did sterling work after air raids. This group (Messrs Gough, Sinden, Hoadley and Homewood) pose with their Wolseley. Note the high visibility white paint on bumper and mudguards, the blackout shields on the headlights and the four stacking metal stretchers on the roof.

63.   Rather more problematical than mole-hills were these craters on Eastbourne's Saffron's Cricket Pitch, left after the Luftwaffe had passed this way in July 1940.

64.   This was the result when a 250 Kg bomb scored a direct hit on the Berkeley Club in Trinity Place on October 8th 1940.

→ 65.   On Friday 13th September 1940, a Dornier 17 scattered high explosive bombs across the town.   One exploded in Seaside near the Recreation Ground and set fire to the gas main, here seen blazing as the Eastbourne Fire Brigade attempt to keep the flames in check. Another bomb cratered the Recreation Ground playing fields whilst another buried itself beneath the Seaside pavement bordering the ground and failed to explode. This was detonated in situ after the war.

66. Alongside the A259 on the outskirts of the town, Horst Perez's Messerschmitt 109 sits guarded by soldiers. Beyond, lies East Dean village. The poles and cables across the field are the familiar anti-glider obstructions of the period. This aeroplane, having been shipped later to the USA and Canada, was "rescued" in the 1960s and brought back to England for restoration and is currently preserved near Bournemouth.

67. This close-up of the tail of Perez's Messerschmitt is painted with five "kill" markings depicting victories over allied aircraft; two Dutch, one French and two British. The 30th September 1940, saw the end of the road for number 1190. There would be no more tallies painted on its fin!

68-69. Interrupted by an air raid warning, this couple signed the register in the shelter situated beneath All Saints Church during their wedding on 15th August 1940.

70. Photographer Harry Deal poses with the smashed up pieces of a Messerschmitt 110 in the grounds of Aldro School on 16th August 1940.

71. Meanwhile, Sub-Officer Pat Short lowers the body of its pilot from the roof of "Hillbrow" in Gaudick Road where he had fallen with an unopened parachute.

impacting into the grounds of Aldro School. Its pilot, Ernst Hollekamp, had abandoned his aircraft too late and fallen with an unopened parachute onto the roof of Hillbrow School whilst his gunner, Richard Schurk, baled out into the sea and drowned.

Within the space of a few months, the war had visited Eastbourne with an awful vengeance and yet only one year earlier, on the outbreak of war, London children had been evacuated here as a safe haven away from the capital!

72-73. The first evacuees leave Eastbourne Station in July 1940 for new homes in Hertfordshire and Bedfordshire. Mayor Arthur Rush sees them off.

74. Yet again, another "unlucky 13", this time the machine of Unteroffizier Schultz down near Langney on 30th September 1940. Like the Messerschmitt 109 down the same day at East Dean, this aircraft also had four victories marked up on its tail.

EAST GRINSTEAD URBAN DISTRICT

Surely the town's most notable claim to fame was the work carried out by pioneering plastic surgeon Sir Archibald McIndoe at the Queen Victoria Hospital. Here, badly burned pilots had their hands, faces and bodies rebuilt by the great surgeon as the battle in which they had so recently participated raged on above them. The "Guinea Pigs" as they became known, were a familiar and accepted sight around the town whilst the work of the hospital became, and is, world famed.

The first bombs in the area fell at 3am on 3rd June 1940, when two were dropped just outside the district at Forest Row, the shattering explosions shaking the folk of East Grinstead from their sleep. Fortunately, there were no casualties, but it was a different story when, on 26th October, a bomb demolished "Stanney" in Holtye Road killing one of the young nurses from the East Grinstead Burns Unit. Luckier were the residents of a house at North End which was cut in half as Junkers Ju88 bomber was shot down onto it on 26th September. Mr Angus Simpson and his family escaped unharmed, but three of its crew were killed, the fourth baling out into captivity. Two other aircraft, a Spitfire and a Hurricane, came down in the district during the battle but both pilots were safe.

HAILSHAM RURAL DISTRICT

The market town of Hailsham was one of many prime strategic defence positions in the South of England which, had invasion come, would have become fortresses encircled with barbed wire, "dragons teeth" defences and road blocks. Later, these locations became known as Nodal Points, officially described thus:-

"A defended locality, situated usually at strategically important road junctions, garrisoned normally by local Home Guards, with the addition of any available troops stationed in the vicinity, and intended to restrict, delay or hamper the operation of enemy invaders until reserves and reinforcements can be brought up".

Such was Hailsham's planned role, with total self-sufficiency intended for one week.

Hailsham, too, had another wartime role in the form of producing full-size replica Hurricane aircraft. These wooden Hurricanes were built by Green Brothers in Western Road, a total of some 500 being made for distribution as decoys on dummy airfields to deceive the Luftwaffe!

Some of the earliest bombs to drop in the region fell at Streeton's Nurseries, Vines Cross, on 17th July, whilst Hailsham itself was hit on August 16th as raiders scattered high explosive bombs across the region. Green Brother's replica Hurricane workshops were slightly damaged and coal scattered far and wide as another bomb hit the coal dump at Knights Nurseries in Ersham Road, whilst a gas main was set alight in Windsor Road. At the Station Road Brickyard (now the Industrial Estate), twenty year old Alfred Lucas was killed as he investigated a delayed-action bomb. The resultant crater formed a pond which marked the spot for many years.

Some of the most exciting "dog fighting" of the entire battle took place over the area on 27th September, as Messerschmitt 110's were pursued homewards across Sussex at treetop height by RAF fighters. Several were brought down in the county and others off the Sussex coast. The most dramatic incident reached a climatic end at Hailsham as one of the Hurricanes of 249 Squadron flown by a young South African, Flying Officer Percy Burton, ran out of ammunion whilst pursuing the leader of the Messerschmitt Squadron, Hauptmann Horst Liensberger. Determined to down his quarry, Burton rammed the German machine from the sky. The enemy plane, its tail unit severed, plunged into a meadow behind Hamlins Mill in Mill Road, Hailsham whilst the victor, unable to recover from the collision, flew headlong into a massive oak tree at Station Road. Both crewmen in the Messerschmitt perished, as did their 21 year old assailant. Today, the shattered oak tree marks the spot, whilst a road on a nearby housing estate is named Burton Walk in the RAF pilot's honour.

Other incidents, though, had humour - and happier endings! At Blackford Farm, Herstmonceux, a Polish pilot of 249 Squadron made an emergency landing, short of petrol, after a patrol. Stepping from his Hurricane, Sgt. Maciejowski enquired where he was. Exactly how the conversation ran can be imagined as the young Pole with his halting command of English struggled to understand the broad Sussex accents. Next day, his fuel tanks replenished, Maciejowski flew out and back to his airfield base. Upon arrival, his report was entered in the Official Record Book of the unit, reporting that: "Sgt Maciejowski had landed at Lost, near Hailsham ....."!

Tragedy struck again on the night of 2nd November when a bomb fell behind a Southdown Bus at Rushlake Green, hurling it over a bank and hedge, killing five passengers and the conductor. Without doubt, the nightime raids were the most terrifying, when bombers could sometimes be heard circling in the darkness before releasing their loads. Perhaps it was this frightening aspect which reputedly drove some residents of Heathfield to seek nightime shelter in the railway tunnel, thereby emulating the behaviour of Londoners, who sought refuge in the Underground system at this time.

75. This time number 14 - but still unlucky! Unteroffizier Zaunbrecher ended up in a cornfield near Mays Farm, Selmeston, on 12th August 1940, his aeroplane badly shot about and Zaunbrecher himself wounded by machine gun bullets.

76. Leo Zaunbrecher (left) is pictured with his mechanic and his Messerschmitt 109 prior to being shot down at Selmeston on 12th Auugust 1940. Note the red devil emblem on the cowling.

77. When this 16 Squadron Lysander made an emergency landing at Marshfoot Lane, Hailsham, on 13th March 1940, it became bogged down in soft ground and had to be removed by a team from 49 Maintenance Unit, RAF Faygate.

78. South African pilot Fg. Off. Percy Burton courageously rammed his opponent over Hailsham on 27th September 1940, after the ammunition in his Hurricane ran out. The enemy aircraft, a Messerschmitt 110, scattered itself across Simmons Field, Mill Road, smashing the sewage culvert as it fell. (Presumably this was the source of the broken pipe in the foreground). Unfortunately, Percy Burton lost his life when his aeroplane smashed into an oak tree at Station Road.

79. The severed tail shows signs of the ramming by Burton's Hurricane, and, following the tradition of German fighter pilots, is marked up with previous victories. Horst Liensberger and Albert Kopge stood no chance of survival.

Hans Beactold was the pilot of a Messerschmitt 110 shot down at Horam on 27th September 1940.

141

No. of Page in Charge Book _____

No. of Charge _____

Bexhill _____ Division

PERSONAL PROPERTY FOUND ON PRISONER.

Received from Police *Sergt. O Golds.*

the undermentioned Property, viz: (*Property of Hans BECHTHOLD (Unter offizier)*)

Cash £ _____ s. _____ d.   Other Articles: *Identity Card in case,*
1 belt, 1 parachute, 1 flying suit, 1 tooth comb
2 pairs glasses, 1 whistle, 2 pencils, 2 skull helmets,
1 pr scissors, 1 pocket knife, 2 field dressings,
1 package red powder, 1 compass on strap, 1 jerkin

Signature of Officer handing over Property

Name *O. Golds.*

Rank *Sergt. No. 2.*

Signature of { Prisoner _____
{ Warder *J. E. ...*

Date *27. Sept.* 19*40*.

65

HASTINGS COUNTY BOROUGH

More famous for 1066, Hastings again found itself in the front line during 1940 and within six days of the outbreak of war, a taste of war in the air came to the town. An RAF Anson twin engined aircraft got into difficulties on 9th September 1939, and ditched into the sea off Fairlight. Its four crew were rescued and the aircraft was floated ashore to be beached on the Stade, where it aroused a good deal of local curiosity. Almost another year was to pass before there was any degree of air activity which affected the region. Throughout the summer of 1940 there were repeated incidents of bombing and machine gunning in the borough, but the most serious and most tragic occurred on 30th September when, during the height of an air battle, a single high explosive bomb struck the coping on the roof of the Plaza Cinema (now W.H.Smith's) and was deflected into mid-air where it exploded above the Memorial. The effect was devastating and left fourteen dead, twelve seriously injured and twenty-three slightly injured. Despite the high civilian toll during this and other incidents, the people of Hastings were nevertheless inspired by the deeds of the RAF's fighter pilots who were daily seen in action above the town.

Consequently, on 24th August, the "Hastings Spitfire Fund" was launched with Alderman A.Blackman JP offering £1000 to the fund if the town could find the balance of £4000 inside one month. The challenge was met, and on 25th September the Minister for Aircraft Production sent a receipt to Hastings for £5000. Within a short space of time a Spitfire named "Hastings" was in service.

As if to celebrate this event, the 25th September saw the timely destruction of a Messerschmitt 110 by a Spitfire on the outskirts of the town. The aircraft crashed astride Beeneys Lane, Baldslow, just off The Ridge and burst into flames as it came to rest. Both of the crew, Eberhard Weyergang and Gustav Nelson, perished in the crash and joined the growing numbers of British and

German military casualties buried in Heroes Corner at the town cemetery. Today, their graves may still be seen there, carefully tended and surrounded by rose bushes and shrubs, side by side with former enemies. Most of the Luftwaffe's wartime casualties were exhumed post-war from locations around Sussex for re-burial in a German Military Cemetery at Cannock Chase, Staffordshire.

Apart from the incident with the Messerschmitt 110, there were several British aircraft down in the locality. On 12th October, a Hurricane was shot down into Coghurst Wood, Guestling, its pilot baling out with gunshot wounds and being treated at the town's Buchanan Hospital.

81. High and dry on The Stade at Hastings is this Anson which had ditched off Fairlight on 9th September 1939. In the distance is the East Hill.

82. The people of Hastings subscribed £5000 to buy a Spitfire, which bore the name of the town.

80. As the German Army began to roll in its "Blitzkrieg" across France on 10th May 1940, the Luftwaffe was, at that moment, photographing the South Coast in its forward planning for "Operation Sealion", the invasion of England. This is Hastings as viewed by the German Air Force.

83. Burnt out and astride Beeney's Lane off The Ridge, Hastings, this Messerschmitt 110 had been chased all the way back from Enfield before being downed. Crewmen Gustav Nelson and Eberhard Weyergang perished in their aeroplane on 25th September 1940.

HORSHAM RURAL DISTRICT

Before the Battle of Britain proper had begun, and with the Battle of France still being fought, the first casualty of the air war in the Horsham Rural District area was the loss of a Hurricane of 145 Squadron in a flying accident at Cowfold on 21st April, which claimed the life of Pilot Officer Gordon-Wilson. Just over two months later, on 27th June, an obsolete Gloster Gladiator biplane fighter ended up on the ground at Lower Beeding, but this time the pilot, Flt. Lt. Bartlett of 53 Squadron, was reported as "safe". Safe in captivity were the entire crew of four who rode their shot-up Junkers Ju88 down to a forced landing at Newells Farm, Nuthurst, on 9th September, whilst on the same day Karl Born had no chance to escape from his doomed Messerschmitt 109 when it crashed a flaming wreck at Roman Gate, Rudgwick. A similar fate befell Alfred Lenz who died from serious injuries when he attempted to force-land at Plummers Plain, near Horsham, on 29th October after having been engaged in combat by Pilot Officer Marsland flying a Hurricane of 253 Squadron. No doubt the losses of these enemy machines helped to bolster the local Spitfire Fund, eventually the required £5,000

was raised and Spitfire No. W3327 became the gift of the area, proudly named "Horsham & District".

Based within the Rural District at Faygate was No. 49 Maintenance Unit, RAF, although in reality its title was something of a misnomer! Charged with the salvage of wrecked aircraft, British and German, from the length and breadth of Southern England the 49 MU Depot became a collecting post for scrap aircraft beyond any hope of further maintenance! Vast mountains of wreckage were assembled here before being taken out by rail to be re-processed and melted down for re-use by the aircraft industry.

Sometimes before they became alloy ingots the German aeroplanes were taken out from Faygate and transported around the country for display purposes raising monies for local Spitfire Funds, War Weapons Weeks etc. Also, it was from Faygate that the Brighton based haulage contractor, A.V.Nicholls & Co., took, their instructions and delivered the wrecks. Faygate's role in clearing the debris of war from across South East England became an important one. The men of the 49 MU were rarely idle!

85. Made in Germany .... finished in England! These unidentifiable piles of mangled aircraft wreckage are the intermingled carcasses of British and German warplanes lost in battles across Sussex and collected together in the dump of 49 Maintenance Unit, RAF Faygate.

86. Next stop Faygate for this Messerschmitt 109 being transported by A. V. Nicholls & Co.

◄— **84.** With its back broken and looking rather sorry for itself, this Junkers 88 ended its days at Newells Farm, Nuthurst, on 9th September 1940, although all the crew survived. Souvenir hunters have stripped the tail of its swastika panels and one of these lies against the engine to the left of the picture.

87.   Taken at Faygate, this engine cowling originates from the Messerschmitt 109 of Leo Zaunbrecher, shot down on 12th August 1940, near Selmeston.   In this posed shot Cpl. Anson "pretends" to be removing the devil emblem, although in actual fact it had been partly removed by souvenir hunters whilst on a lorry during an overnight stop at Lydney, Glos. on an exhibition tour of Cardiff, Birmingham, Manchester and Glasgow.   LAC. Cookson gives the "thumbs up"!

88. Another shot at Faygate with the lorry and trailer of Nicholls & Co carrying yet more scrap from wrecked enemy aircraft. On the trailer is a float from a Heinkel 59 seaplane whilst the lorry carries a Junkers Jumo engine, prop blades and Heinkel 111 wing section. Posing to the left of the group is Mr. A. V. Nicholls, haulage contractor.

HORSHAM URBAN DISTRICT

Horsham's main role during the Battle of Britain was as home to Head Quarters of No. 2 Group, Royal Observer Corps.   Here, vital information from Observer Corps posts scattered across the region was sifted and filtered for onward transmission to RAF Fighter Command from the H Q in Dene Road.

Without doubt, the work carried out by the Observer Corps played an important and significant part in events of 1940.

Sadly, three young children were amongst the fatal casualties when bombs hit Orchard Road on 29th November which, in total, resulted in seven deaths.

HOVE MUNICIPAL BOROUGH

Shortly after the outbreak of war in September 1939, Hove Town Hall became the focus of attention as the Allied Supreme War Council met there in secret. Included in this illustrious gathering were Mr Neville Chamberlain, M. Daladier (the French Premier), Lord Halifax and General Gamelin of the French Army. Within the span of one year the French Army had caved in, Chamberlain had gone and the pace of war had changed beyond anything discussed at that meeting when Hove was far from being a front line town!

On 30th August, just as many Hove residents were settling down to lunch, an air battle developed overhead as Hurricanes from Tangmere engaged Heinkel HeIII bombers with their fighter escort. As the planes wheeled and dived high above amidst the sound of chattering machine guns, one of the Hurricanes was seen to tilt earthwards. A few moments later it was in a near vertical dive at full throttle; its howling headlong passage being a terrifying ordeal for those on the ground below. Eventually, it impacted with ground adjacent to the eastern footpath of Woodhouse Road and on the boundary of waste land to the east of Portland Gate. The force of the impact blasted a crater in the pavement and drove the wreckage deep into the earth. It was assumed that its young pilot, Sgt. Denis Noble of 43 Squadron and a native of Retford, had been killed in mid-air as he made no attempt to abandon his stricken machine. Just two weeks prior to his death, Denis Noble had written home: "I still fly Hurricanes and would not change for anything. I think that they are marvellous machines and would take anything in one". Today, nothing remains to show where the fighter crashed, but its engine and much of the fuselage still lies buried some fifteen feet below the pavement of Woodhouse Road.

89. This water filled pit in the pavement at the junction of Hove was caused by the crash of Sgt. Noble's Hurricane on 30th August 1940. Virtually the entire aeroplane was driven deep underground by the force of the 400 mph impact. Even so, the scene attracts a good number of sightseers! Published at the time the picture was captioned as "the end of a Hun fighter!" Censorship would not have allowed any indication that this was the scene of a RAF loss.

LEWES MUNICIPAL BOROUGH

One of the most unusual events of the Battle of Britain in Sussex occurred on 28th August, 1940, when a Gotha bi-plane which had become lost in Channel fog was forced to land near Lewes racecourse by two Hurricanes. Its young pilot, Leonard Buckle, was quickly taken into captivity whilst his intact aeroplane was flown away by the RAF who subsequently repainted the aircraft in British markings and test flew it before transferring it to Maintenance Command.

Like most other towns in the region, Lewes was subject to air attack, but despite several incidents during 1940 there were no fatal casualties. The town had a lucky escape on 5th October when a string of eight bombs was dropped from Cliffe Hill to the Cattle Market and between Southover Churchyard and the railway line to Brighton. Of these, two failed to explode but one on Chapel Hill was successfully dealt with although the other one in the garden of Southover Grange was rather more problematical! With the Winterbourne Stream running close by, the bomb simply sank deeper and deeper as attempts were made to extricate it. Eventually, the effort was abandoned and the bomb covered in with concrete. Presumably, the missile remains entombed to this day!

On 11th September, amidst the sound of much machine-gunning, a Messerschmitt 109 appeared heading south at low level, hotly pursued by a Hurricane. The chase ended at Houndean Bottom, just above the Brighton Road, where the German aircraft plunged burning into a field, carrying its experienced pilot, Hauptmann Ernst Wiggers, to his death. Meanwhile, his victor, Sgt. William Higgins of 253 Squadron, circled the billowing black, funeral pyre momentarily before heading off and seeking further action (Sadly, Sgt Higgins was killed in action three days later). More fortunate that his German counterpart, Pilot Officer T.S. "Wimpey" Wade escaped unhurt when his Spitfire of 92 Squadron turned over during a forced landing on the Race Course. Sad to relate, Wade was to lose his life in a post war flying accident near Lewes when the Hawker P1081 jet he was test flying crashed at Ringmer on 3rd April, 1951.

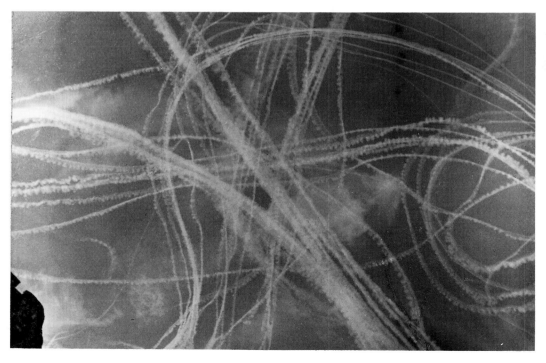

91. The smoking ruins of Hptm. Wiggers Messerschmitt 109 at Houndean Bottom, Lewes, as the wreck burns itself out on 11th September 1940. Beyond can be seen the Brighton Road (A27) and the Lewes to Brighton Railway line.

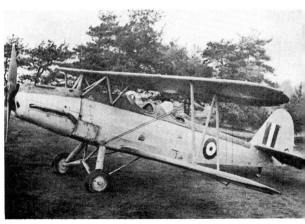

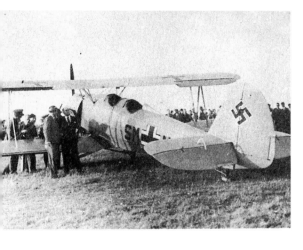

92. This was another of the captured Luftwaffe machines which landed in Sussex and which subsequently saw service in the RAF. This time the unusual prize was a Gotha 145 communications bi-plane lost over the Channel and forced down by fighters on Lewes racecourse.

93. The Gotha was repainted for use by the RAF.

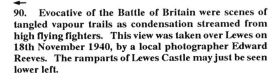

90. Evocative of the Battle of Britain were scenes of tangled vapour trails as condensation streamed from high flying fighters. This view was taken over Lewes on 18th November 1940, by a local photographer Edward Reeves. The ramparts of Lewes Castle may just be seen lower left.

LITTLEHAMPTON URBAN DISTRICT

As the Battle of Britain got into its stride, the imagination of the British public was captured by the exploits of the RAF's fighter pilots and the exciting sleek lines of the Spitfire. Capitalising on this adulation, the authorities were quick to encourage the public to contribute to locally organised "Spitfire Funds" where towns and communities collected money for presentation aircraft, £5,000 being the purchase price. As he launched the Littlehampton fund on August 16th, Mr C.J.Gladden (Chairman of Littlehampton Urban District Council) encouraged the good citizens of Littlehampton to participate in the pleasure and privilege of helping to buy a Spitfire. Two days later the fund was given a boost! As smoke rose from the heavily bombed airfield at Ford, one of the attacking Junkers Ju87 "Stuka" dive bombers circled and landed on the fairway at Ham Manor Golf Course. A few bullet holes and a flat tyre belied the real reason for its arrival as the pilot vainly sought medical aid for his gunner who had been hit by machine gun fire. Unfortunately, he was beyond help. As the Stuka sat on the Golf Course it attracted much attention from sightseers, even the local Home Guard unit being photographed proudly alongside. As time passed, it became the focus of attention for souvenir hunting on a grand scale, being pillaged, plundered and looted. Machine guns were taken away, instruments and controls ripped from the cockpit and the swastikas and crosses torn from the wings, fuselage and tail. Such was the scale of the theft which went on, that by the time an RAF pilot arrived to fly away the prize for evaluation only a shabby and by now partially burnt out hulk remained - fit only for the scrapyard!

The Heinkel HeIII which was shot down at Hellyers Farm, Wick, on 26th August fared somewhat better and was removed more or less intact before being robbed in the same fashion. Captain of the aircraft, Ignatz Krenn, was captured unharmed by a farmer armed with nothing more potent than his walking stick! Later, in his POW Camp, Krenn a talented cartoonist, depicted his downfall and capture in humorous vein - all five crewmen

being fortunate to survive their ordeal!

These two arrivals, then, must have helped the local Spitfire fund. So, too, must the satisfying fact that no British aircraft were lost in the administrative district during 1940.

94. Shot down by fighters onto Hellyers Farm, Wick, this was the Heinkel 111 of Ignatz Krenn after is unscheduled arrival on English soil on 26th August 1940.

74

95. As he is marched off into captivity, Oblt. Krenn attracts local curiosity at Chichester railway station. Nevertheless, he looks calm, composed and dignified in his smart uniform with leather gloves, riding breeches and flying boots.

96. Oblt . Krenn's Heinkel 111 makes its last journey by road away from Hellyers Farm, Wick, after being shot down there by Hurricanes of 43 Squadron from Tangmere on 26th August 1940.

97. Snapped illicitly from Littlehampton Station this picture shows a Douglas Boston aircraft circling from RAF Ford where the first examples of this new American aircraft were in service by October 1940, one of them being destroyed there in an air raid on the 8th of that month. The photographer was observed in this clandestine act and had his camera and film confiscated. When developed by the Police, this was the result - hardly something which could have been regarded a threat to national security!

98-99. Souvenir hunting on an elaborate scale helped to reduce this Junkers 87 Stuka from an almost intact and undamaged example to a mere hulk after it was brought down at Ham Manor Golf Course on 18th August, 1940; but first the local Home Guard pose with their trophy!

MIDHURST RURAL DISTRICT

Whilst the area saw its share of random bombings, it was fortunate in that not one single fatal casualty resulted from enemy action during 1940. Nevertheless, a furious air battle raged over the district on 13th August, resulting in the loss of two RAF Hurricanes and a Junkers Ju88 bomber. Shot down over Cocking, Flt. Lt. Tom Dalton Morgan took to his parachute leaving his aeroplane to explode on impact with Cocking Down, whilst at Northend Farm, Stedham, Pilot Officer Tony Woods-Scawen force landed his Hurricane which was subsequently destroyed by fire, despite efforts by the local fire brigade to save it by shovelling soil over the burning engine. Both aeroplanes and pilots were from the Tangmere based 43 Squadron, but to redress the balance somewhat, one of the enemy bombers was sent hurtling into the ground at Philliswood, Treyford, where it exploded and burnt out amongst the trees. Before it fell, three of the crew baled out into captivity, but a fourth crewman, Oberleutnant Josef Oestermann, failed to escape. The impact and fire were so intense that no trace of Oestermann was ever found and thus he has no known grave. In recent years his family have placed a simple memorial to this young airman close to the spot where he died.

In November, on the 24th, an RAF Whitley bomber returning from a long-range night raid on Turin, Italy, crashed at Elsted Manor Farm and burnt out having run out of fuel before managing to reach an airfield. All of the crew abandoned the aircraft safely. Before the year was out, two more British aircraft had come down in the region during December. On the 12th a Gypsy Moth ended up at Halfway Bridge, Lodsworth, and a Miles Magister at Filtsham Farm, Cocking, on Christmas Eve. The pilots of both planes were safe.

100. This was a Junkers 88 in Phillis Wood, Treyford on 13th August 1940. All that exists and which is identifiable amongst the ash and molten aluminium are two cylinder liners and a propeller blade. Once again, the local schoolboy population wait to fill their pockets when the backs of the army guards are turned. A brisk trade in perspex, shrapnel, bullets and aircraft parts was very much in vogue at this time amongst young boys.

101. Oberleutnant Osterman was captain of the aircraft downed at Treyford on 13th August 1940, although no trace of him has even been found. In recent years a memorial close to the spot of his death has been erected by his family.

NEWHAVEN URBAN DISTRICT

With its important role as a port, it was inevitable that Newhaven would be singled out for attention and one of the first and most serious raids took place on 11th October when eight high explosive bombs and one oil bomb were dropped in Saxon Road, Brighton Road and on the Newhaven Convent where one of the sisters was killed and a number injured. It was on the night of 28th October, however, that a rather more serious attempt at hitting Newhaven hard was made by seventeen Junkers Ju88s. As they circled the town three incendiary markers were dropped before the bombers dropped their loads and machine gunned the area. One bomb demolished 56 South Road, leaving an Anderson air raid shelter perched on the edge of the huge crater which had once been the house. Twelve people had sought refuge in the shelter, but sadly nine year old May Bollen was killed by the effects of blast. Tragedy again hit the town on 11th December, when a single 500 Kg bomb caused twelve fatalities at Folly Field, Lewes Road. To redress the balance somewhat, a number of enemy aircraft were seen to be brought down in the sea throughout the period and a Dornier was shot down just outside the district at Tarring Neville on 22nd November although during the height of the battle itself, a Hurricane was shot down over Newhaven, crashing onto a fence at New Road as its pilot parachuted to safety.

PETWORTH RURAL DISTRICT

The most dramatic incident to occur in this district during the Battle of Britain took place on 16th August when a Heinkel HeIII was shot down over Kirdford by a Hurricane of No. 1 Squadron flown by an Israeli, Pilot Officer Goodman. As the bomber fell earthwards, one of its wings parted company from the rest of the aircraft which fell like a falling sycamore seed, both engines roaring, until it crashed into a field at Upper Frithfold Farm. It was followed by the severed wing which fluttered and soared until it plunged into woodland at Belchambers Farm. Moments later, and as Goodman circled the wreckage, the bomb load exploded sending wreckage far and wide damaging Goodman's engine, forcing him to beat a hasty retreat to his Northolt base! None of the four crew members stood any chance of survival and today the crater caused by the tremendous explosion is a tranquil Sussex pond which marks the passing of an aircraft and four young lives.

On 30th September, another air battle raged over the district and a Messerschmitt 109 was sent diving into Jays Copse at Roundhurst Farm, Northchapel, after Hauptmann Walter Kienzle had taken to his parachute, seriously wounded. In the same battle one of his comrades was also shot down. Seriously burnt, Leutnant Herbert Schmidt descended by parachute near Kingsley Green whilst his Messerschmitt 109 broke up in mid air, falling in pieces across the Surrey border near Haslemere. Schmidt, meanwhile, recovered from his injuries and spent the remainder of the war as prisoner. As the battle drew to its conclusion there was a rather less dramatic loss of a British aircraft in the form of a Tiger Moth of No. 13 Elementary Flying Training School, which came down at Petworth.

102. This was the largest piece of wreckage when the Heinkel 111 exploded at Upper Frithfold Farm on 16th August 1940. The resulting crater in the background is now a pond.

PORTSLADE URBAN DISTRICT

On the morning of 21st March 1940, an RAF Blenheim en-route from France to Tangmere crossed the coast near Shoreham at about 400ft with undercarriage lowered in accordance with the recognition and identification procedures then in operation. Almost immediately, it vanished into a thick bank of fog and shortly afterwards struck the Downs between Mile Oak Farm and Fulking, breaking up and catching fire as it slithered through gorse bushes. The pilot and observer were killed immediately, but one of the passengers, Cpl. Lapwood, managed to struggle free just as three men arrived on the scene. One of them, Mr Gerald Winter, clambered into the burning wreckage and rescued the gunner, LAC Oultram, thereby saving his life. For this act of gallantry Mr Winter was subsequently awarded the George Medal.

Throughout the summer of 1940, daily air battles were fought out over Portslade, but on 10th October two Spitfires of 92 Squadron collided over the town during an attack on German bombers. It seems that one of the pilots, Flying Officer John Drummond, was hit and wounded by machine gunfire. As his aircraft wobbled out of the fray and the injured Drummond attempted to abandon his aeroplane, it struck another Spitfire flown by Pilot Officer Desmond Williams. Drummond's aeroplane plunged into Jubilee Field at the junction of East Hill Drive and East Hill Way. Drummond, who had baled out too low, was killed, so too was his comrade, Desmond Williams, who perished when his aeroplane fell in neighbouring Hove. This tragedy marked the end of the Battle of Britain for Portslade, but highlighted the human cost of the ultimate victory won by RAF Fighter Command.

RYE MUNICIPAL BOROUGH

Although the smallest administrative district in the county, war, nevertheless, did not pass it by! Had invasion come, then the flat marshland to its south would doubtless have swarmed with the infantry and tanks of the Wehrmacht; the historic old town perched on its mound overlooking the surrounding district would probably have been a heavily contested strategic point. As it turned out, the Battle of Britain came to Rye with a vengeance.

On August 18th 1940, Dornier 17 bombers returning from a raid on RAF Kenley overflew the town, harried by British fighters. As they passed twenty- eight 50 Kg bombs were released destroying eleven houses and seriously damaging eleven more. Three people were killed in this incident and another three injured. With the smoke still rising from a "blitzed" Rye, a young German airman who had been shot down across the border in Kent was brought into the Memorial Hospital. Despite tender care by the doctors and nurses he died shortly after. A plaque near the scene of one of the bombing incidents on 18th August 1940, now records the events of that day. It was a day which subsequent research shows to have been the hardest fought of the entire battle, although Sunday 15th September 1940 remains nationally remembered as "Battle of Britain Day".

Some days prior to the bombing of Rye, the town experienced the crump of exploding bombs as, on 12th August, Messerschmitt 110s attempted to knock out the RAF Radar Station to the east of the town.

It was known as RAF Rye, or more correctly, Air Ministry Experimental Station Rye. As the smoke cleared from the bomb bursts the massive transmitter and receiver masts were seen to be intact, but today all that remains of the station are a few concrete block-houses and the bases of the masts.

To redress the balance, the citizens of Rye were cheered on 11th September to see two billowing black columns of smoke rising from the direction of East Guldeford. What they watched were the funeral pyres of two Heinkel HeIII bombers which had been forced down and then set on fire by their crews. Aside from this incident, and numerous other aircraft down in the immediate locality, no aeroplanes actually fell within the boundaries of Rye Municipal Borough.

103. These 360 foot transmitting masts towered above the Chain Home Radar stations at Rye, Pevensey and Poling and played a vital part in winning the Battle of Britain. Shrouded in secrecy, the radar stations were euphemistically called Air Ministry Experimental Stations, but many of the locals were convinced of their real purpose - to emit "death rays" towards enemy bombers and stop their engines. More than one motorist told how that his car had mysteriously cut out when driving near the masts!

104. These twin columns of smoke mark the flaming ends of two bombers, Heinkel 111's, shot down near East Guldeford and set ablaze by their crews on 11th September 1940.

105. Just before breakfast time on 13th August 1940, Oberleutnant Paul Temme was forced to land his disabled Messerschmitt 109 in a stubble field just across the railway line from Shoreham airport. In the background can be seen the camouflaged hangars, terminal building and control tower. Later, this photograph was censored prior to publication and the buildings obliterated from the skyline.

SEAFORD URBAN DISTRICT

Although no aircraft either enemy or friendly came down within the district during 1940, the town was not without its moments of drama during the Battle of Britain. One of the earliest episodes was when, on 18th August, a group of Dornier 17 bombers roared over the town en-route for Kenley, passing overhead at little more than treetop height. Later, on 26th August, a stick of thirteen high explosive bombs fell across gound near Seaford Head and the Senior School, but there were no casualties. The town was again fortunate on 5th October, when a single but very large bomb detonated on the Crouch Football Field, close to Bramber Road blasting a crater some 30ft in diameter and 15ft deep, but otherwise causing comparatively little damage. Luck was again on the side of Seaford when ten bombs were dropped in a line from Corsica Road to the Parish Church, but with damage being restricted to a broken tombstone and a damaged shed at the rear of the Plough Inn.

SHOREHAM URBAN DISTRICT

Apart from Tangmere, Ford and Thorney Island the only other pre-war airfield in the county of any significance and which was used during 1940 was Shoreham. However, its use was primarily restricted to operations by Lysanders of 225 Squadrom on anti-invasion coastal patrols looking out for fleets of German landing craft. Later, operational Beaufighter aircraft of the Fighter Interception Unit took up residence here, but possibly the most exciting episode was when, early on the morning of 13th August 1940, a Messerschmitt 109 was shot down and made a forced landing in a stubble field at New Salts Farm, just across the railway line from the aerodrome. Its pilot, Oberleutnant Paul Temme of the famous "Richthofen" squadron clambered unharmed from the cockpit of his intact fighter and his aeroplane later subjected to much photography. Post war, Paul Temme's account of the incident was pub-lished, describing how that the aeroplane ended up on its back, a complete wreck and with its wings torn off! As evidenced by the pictures, this was not exactly the case. The camera does not lie!

Although the aerodrome, Shoreham Harbour and the nearby power station must all have presented tempting targets, there was, nevertheless, comparatively little serious bombing in 1940. However, five fatalities were caused by enemy action at the Shoreham Shipping Company Wharf on 21st October. The Ministry of Home Security reports for the night of 28th/29th November talk of "No serious consequences" when bombs fell on Shoreham. Perhaps it was one of these bombs, a 250Kg device, which was found on the airfield during the 1980s. Defused, the bomb is now displayed in the terminal building at Shoreham Airport.

SOUTHWICK URBAN DISTRICT

This small district saw no aeroplanes actually downed within its boundaries but a particularly harrowing incident took place here on 8th October, when three low flying Heinkel HeIIIs crossed the coast, machine gunned Southwick and released twenty four high explosive bombs into a residential area. Although three failed to explode, one bungalow was destroyed, a store building burnt out, one person killed and eight injured. Perhaps some measure of consolation was afforded by the later news that one of the raiders had been brought down at Stansted Park near Chichester.

UCKFIELD RURAL DISTRICT

Before the Battle of Britain had got into its stride, random bombs which dropped across Jarvis Brook on 17th July had struck cottages at Dewsbury Villas, Western Road, causing the tragic death of two year old Doreen Sivers and severely injuring her mother, Martha, who died some time later in Tunbridge Wells Hospital. On the same day, a Lysander crashed near Forest Row, taking the lives of the two airmen on board. From this time onwards, and throughout almost the entire remainder of 1940, air battles and their attendant losses became regular events. On 15th August, Messerschmitt 110s of the German Er.Gr.210 unit with their Messerschmitt 109 escorts were being pursued back across Sussex after a hard hitting raid on Croydon aerodrome, when the CO's Messerschmitt 110 was shot down in a mass of flames at Bletchinglye Farm, Rotherfield. Hauptmann Walter Rubensdorffer and his gunner, Richard Kretzer, both died as the blazing twin engined plane smashed itself to pieces in a piggery. Meanwhile, a few miles away to the

106. "Cor ..... there's a Messerschmitt in the garden, Mum!" With its sharks teeth almost knocked out on the garden fence this bedraggled Messerschmitt 110 ended up on the lawn at Little Butts Farm, Cousley Wood on 4th September 1940, shortly after lunch. Both crew walked away - shaken but unharmed.

north, Ltn. Horst Marx drifted down on his parachute, having vainly tried to protect his commanding officer before being hit and forced to bale out. Marx landed with little more than a cut thumb while his Messerschmitt 109 thumped into the ground at Lightlands Farm, Frant.

The following day, German bombers again returned to the area and whilst being pursued southwards released a stick of bombs across the area from above the clouds. One unlucky hit found its mark on James Berry's Scocoe's Farm, Hadlow Down, just as his two sons James and Alfred were finishing off their milking. Both were killed, along with thirteen cows, as a total of no less than seventy one high explosive bombs rained across the locality.

Losses of aircraft, British and German, continued unabated and drama surrounded each incident as it occurred. On 4th September, the occupants of Little Butts Farm House were surprised to see a Messerschmitt 110 slithering across the ground towards them, eventually coming to rest in the garden as its two crewmen clambered out. Somehow, the warlike sharks mouth painted on its nose looked strangely ineffectual and impotent as the aeroplane sat on the lawn of an English country garden! Sunday 15th September is remembered nationally as Battle of Britain day and the residents of Rotherfield had cause to remember for it was the day when a Dornier 17 swooped low overhead, burning furiously and with a pursuing Hurricane firing remorselessly. One of the crew attempted to bale out, but his parachute fouled on the tail-plane and the unfortunate airman was dragged to his death along with his three comrades as the bomber smashed into the ground near the Bicycle Arms Public House. Such were the horrors of war, horrors to which the civilian population were now exposed on a daily basis.

Attempting no doubt to escape from such frightfulness, artist Edmund Wimperis sat and painted the pleasant pastoral scene at Tablehurst Farm, Forest Row, on 30th September, capturing on his canvas the early Autumn hues. As he painted, a Hurricane fighter hurtled out of a dog fight above and smashed into the ground not many yards in front of his easel. With a sense of history, Wimperis painted in what little wreckage of the aeroplane remained above ground. Victim of this episode was one of the comparatively few Australians to participate in the Battle of Britain, Pilot Officer John Dallas Crossman.

As the battle drew to its conclusion, one of the last casualties was the pilot of a Messerschmitt 109 shot down at Mayfield Flat, Cross-in-Hand, on 7th October. Paul Lege, a veteran of some 48 operational flights over England, could not escape from his aeroplane before it crashed. Like Crossman, he would never see his native land again.

107. Target Farnborough ..... destination Blackboys, Sussex. This is how a Heinkel 111 ended up - smashed to pieces in a field at Roy Hill on 30th August 1940. Some of the crew parachuted out and one was apprehended by Home Guardsman Ted Blunt, later congratulated by his C.O.

108. Uffz. Lege poses confidently with his trusty Messerschmitt 109 on an airfield in France, but very soon this aeroplane would carry Paul Lege to his death at Mayfield Flats, near Hadlow Down, on 7th October 1940, when shot down by a Hurricane.

109. This particular Dornier 17 of 9/KG.76 was also doomed to end up smashed to bits over England. F1+AT was shot down in flames near the Bicycle Arms, Rotherfield, on Battle of Britain Sunday, 15th September 1940.

→ 110. "I heard a noise like a pea on a tin plate" wrote Oblt. Bode when describing the moment his Messerschmitt 109 engine was hit by a lucky (or unlucky!) bullet strike during a mission to escort bombers over London on 9th September 1940. Turning for home, Knowle Farm, Mayfield, was as far as he got before the engine overheated.

→ 111. After Gunther Bode's Messerschmitt 109 - E No. 1394 crash-landed at "Knowle", Mayfield, Sussex on 9th September 1940, it was put on display at Stanhays Garage, Ashford, Kent.

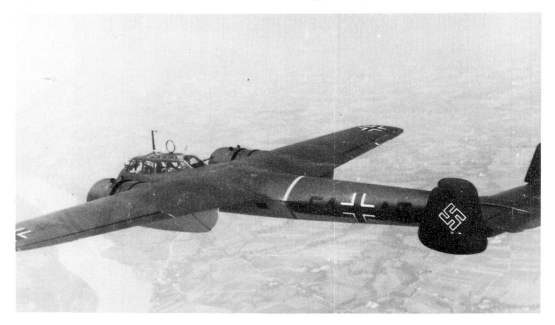

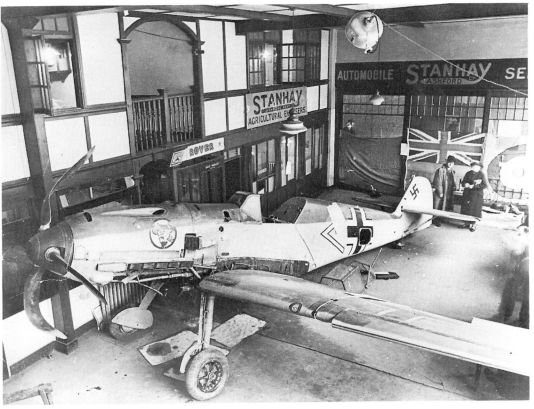

WORTHING MUNICIPAL BOROUGH

When Flt.Lt.John Simpson was shot down off Worthing on 19th July and baled out of his week-old Hurricane, he descended on his parachute to land in a back garden in the town. Those familiar with the 1968 classic film "Battle of Britain" will recall the scene where actor Edward Fox lands by parachute through the greenhouse of an English backgarden. The scene which developed is strangely reminiscent of Simpson's own account of his adventure: "..... and then I hit the roof of a house ..... the next thing I was going through a fence backwards, and then, bang into a cucumber frame! It was a little house and garden. A woman came running and brought me tea and then a policeman with a glass of whisky. He was in the street and handed it over the garden wall ..... then a woman pushed a little boy forward and said "Ernie, give the gentleman those cigarettes!" .... he came running up to me saying that when he grew up, he wanted to be an airman too!" It would be nice to think that Ernie's aspirations were met. However, on scanning the Civilian War Dead Register for Worthing one is tempted to contemplate over an entry for the following year: "FOULGER. Ernest Kenneth, age 16, of 84 Haynes Road. Killed 1st November, 1941". Could this be our same Ernie?

On 4th September, following a fierce battle when several Messerschmitt 110s were shot down to the north of the town, one of the victorious RAF pilots made an emergency landing with his damaged aircraft at Goring. Flying Officer Jankiewicz, a Pole flying Hurricanes with the Tangmere based 601 Squadron, was unhurt in this incident.

The 8th October, like a number of the surrounding districts, also saw attack from three low flying Heinkel HeIIIs. In this attack, 42 Park Road was hit, killing outright 59 year old Helena Hansell and her 20 year old daughter, Ellen. Another victim of the attack was Home Guardsman Robin Kennard, killed as he purchased a packet of cigarettes at a Lyndhurst Road shop.

112. This rabbit became a casualty when a Heinkel 111 was shot down on to waste ground at Honeysuckle Lane, High Salvington, on 16th August 1940. First on the scene was a soldier on leave, Mr. Round, who being fluent in German and wearing civilian clothes was arrested as a suspected spy when the authorities arrived on the scene and found him in the aircraft speaking German to the crew to whom he was rendering assistance.

113. After much interrogation Mr. Round's identity was established and he was allowed to go - unlike the three surviving crewmen who remained in captivity until 1946. Apparently, the aeroplane proved something of an attraction for the local constabulary who all wanted to have their photograph taken on the wreck.

114. This is the bullet-riddled fuselage of the Heinkel at High Salvington. The censorship Bureau have obliterated some of the aircraft code letters on this print for security reasons. Note also the opened paracute on the ground - pulled apart by onlookers. Parachute material was a sought-after wartime commodity for making pillow cases, sheets, underwear and even wedding gowns and christening robes!

115. The severed engine of Oblt. Schiller's Messerschmitt 110 has partly buried itself in the hard earth at High Salvington on 4th September 1940. The souvenir hunters are probably hoping that the tin hatted policeman will go away!

Police Notice

AIR RAID DANGER

CONCEAL YOUR LIGHTS—Precautions to be taken immediately by all concerned

PRIVATE DWELLINGS

All windows, skylights, glazed doors, or other openings must be completely screened after dusk, so that no light is visible from outside.

If blinds are used alone, they must be of stout material and dark in colour and must cover the window completely.   If curtains are used they must be dark and thick.

Dark blankets or carpets or thick sheets of brown paper can be used to cover windows temporarily.

Special care must be taken to cover completely skylights and other windows directly visible from the air.

All lights near a door leading outside the building must be screened so that no light can be seen when the door is opened.

WORTHING RURAL DISTRICT

An intense air battle with Messerschmitt 110 fighters on 4th September resulted in several of these aircraft being brought down across the county and offshore, two of them being within the Worthing Rural District Area at Mill Hill, Shoreham, and at Patching. At Patching, Lt. Muenich force-landed his burning aircraft on the Downs having previously ordered his gunner, Uffz.Kaeser, to bale out of their critically damaged fighter. When Kaeser reported that he could not open the damaged hood to leave the aeroplane, his pilot bravely landed the Messerschmitt, feeling that he could not bale out and leave his colleague to his fate. Slithering to a halt, Muenich jumped out and set about smashing the canopy which was trapping his crewman. Running from the blazing aeroplane the two realised they were quite alone, no civilians, Army or Police had yet turned up! Then, a few miles away, they noticed the sun gleaming on the English Channel. Beyond it lay France and home, but now out of reach ..... or was it? Quickly returning to their smouldering wreck, the enterprising pair retrieved the life saving rubber dinghy, inflated it and legged it across the Downs towards the sea. Suddenly a shot rang out and the two were left holding a limp and useless sheet of yellow rubber. The game was up! As the Army arrived, an officer offered Muenich a warm bottle of beer which the German gratefully accepted. As he drank, the young Luftwaffe pilot, shot down on his first operational flight over England, told the Army Officer how that for Britain the war was as good as lost. Gloomily, the Englishman confided that he agreed with this prediction! Drama, too, surrounded the loss of the Messerschmitt 110 at Mill Hill on Shoreham Downs. After its rough landing the victorious but so far unidentified British pilot landed his Hurricane nearby, supervised the capture of the two crew and then calmly took off from the sloping hillside where he had landed.

Fortunately, and despite several aircraft losses, there was no loss of life or serious injury as the result of RAF aircraft being downed in the vicinity. Some humour surrounded the emergency landing of a Spitfire of 602 Squadron at Norway Farm, Rustington, on 18th August. As it landed it sliced through overhead cables carrying 33,000 volts , coming to rest amidst blue flashes and sparks and severing the power supply to nearby Littlehampton. As the shaken and injured Flying Officer Peter Fergusson emerged from the wreckage, those approaching were convinced he was German ... or certainly foreign. Nobody present could understand the broad Scottish accent, interspersed with Gaelic curses! The story, however, has a sequel. As the result of this incident and his injuries Fergusson was taken off flying and became ADC to the Duke of Kent. Recurring medical problems resulted in Fergusson being sent to see the Duke of Kent's personal physician and while he was undergoing treatment the Duke and his entire entourage were killed in an air crash in Scotland. Fergusson should have been amongst them and thus had a second lucky escape!

Worthy of mention is the radar station at Poling, a vital part of the RAF's defences of the UK and then known as Air Ministry Experimental Station Poling. The huge transmitting and receiving masts have long since been dismantled, but some of the buildings still remain on site and one or two bear the scars of the Luftwaffe's attention on 18th August 1940, when the site came under heavy attack from "Stuka" dive bombers.

Apart from these incidents civilian casualties were inflicted on 10th July (the first "official" day of the Battle of Britain) when bombs were dropped on Framptons Nurseries, East Preston, killing John Marpole and Leslie Clark. The 12th November also saw casualties when three persons were killed at Valley Road, although one of the bombs dropped on this occasion did not explode until 1945!

← 116. Ltn. Muenich made a hazardous landing at Patching in his burning Messerschmitt 110 to save the life of his crewman, Uffz. Kaeser, who was unable to bale out due to damage inflicted on his canopy cover. Both men survived the crash on 4th September 1940.

118. The masts have long since gone, but Air Ministry living quarters (now private houses) still bear the repaired scars made by bomb splinters and gunfire in that raid.

← 117. These are the transmitting and receiving masts at Poling radar station and which came under dive-bombing attack from Junkers 87 Stukas on 18th August 1940.

119. Beachy Head, 1940. For many a Luftwaffe aircrew this was their first sight of England... but their last view of the English Channel! Taken from the cockpit of a Dornier 17 as a raiding force from bomber unit 9/KG.76 roared in at low level on 18th August 1940, to attack RAF Kenley, this picture was taken minutes before photograph nos. 24 and 27. Note the propeller spinner cone.

120. After the battle .... tranquility. Having contemptuously muddied the German cross with paw prints a Sussex Spaniel suns himself on the wing of a downed Junkers 88 in Pagham Harbour on 9th September 1940.

TABLE OF AIRCRAFT DOWN
IN SUSSEX

The figures in the third column refer to the maps on pages 10 to 13.

ARUNDEL MUNICIPAL BOROUGH

13.8.40	Junkers 88		Swanbourne Lake, Arundel
9.9.40	Spitfire		Near Arundel

BATTLE RURAL DISTRICT

10.9.39	Hurricane		Clayton Farm, nr Dallington
10.9.39	"		Newcastle Farm, Dallington
10.9.39	"		Haselden Farm, Dallington
10.9.39	"		Cripps Farm, Dallington
10.9.39	"		Barn Farm, Brightling
21.11.39	"		Pett
13.8.40	Blenheim		Conghurst Wd. nr Sandhurst
15.8.40	M/schmitt 110	C15	School Farm, Hooe
16.8.40	M/schmitt 109		Turzes Farm, Etchingham
24.8.40	"		Broomhill Farm, Camber
29.8.40	Spitfire		Great Wigsell, Hurst Green
29.8.40	M/schmitt 109	C16	New Lodge Farm, Hooe
29.8.40	Hurricane		Camber Castle
29.8.40	"		Underwoods Fm, Etchingham
29.8.40	"	D1	Brigden Hill Fm, Ashburnham
31.8.40	"		Conghurst, nr. Sandhurst
31.8.40	"		Newenden Bridge, Northiam
1.9.40	M/schmitt 109		Newbridge, Iden
1.9.40	"		Strand Bridge, Winchelsea
2.9.40	Hurricane		Near Rye
4.9.40	"		Catts Green, Cripps Corner
6.9.40	Spitfire		Quickbourne Lane, Northiam
6.9.40	"		Pelsham Farm, Peasmarsh
9.9.40	M/schmitt 109		Rosemary Farm, Ticehurst
10.9.40	Spitfire		Hutchings Farm, Etchingham
11.9.40	Heinkel 111		Gate Farm, Staplecross
11.9.40	"		Broomhill Fm, E.Guldeford
11.9.40	"		" "
11.9.40	Hurricane		Lordine Wood, Staplecross
15.9.40	Dornier 17		18 Pounder Fm, Westfield
15.9.40	Hurricane		Church Field, Udimore
15.9.40	Spitfire		Warren Farm, Fairlight
17.9.40	M/schmitt 109		Camber Farm, Camber
25.9.40	M/schmitt 110		Beaulieu Farm, Baldslow
27.9.40	Spitfire		Bivelham, Stonegate
27.9.40	Hurricane	D2	Franchise Manor, Burwash
27.9.40	"	D3	Giffords Farm, Dallington
28.9.40	"		Bewlbridge, Lamberhurst
28.9.40	"	D4	Earlsdown, Dallington
30.9.40	M/schmitt 109		Claytons Farm, Peasmarsh
30.9.40	"		Pelsham Farm, Peasmarsh
4.10.40	Heinkel 111		Gypsum Mines, Netherfield
5.10.40	M/schmitt 109		Lower Gate Farm, Peasmarsh
7.10.40	Spitfire		Baileys Reed Fm, Hurst Green
7.10.40	M/schmitt 109		Lidham Marshes, Guestling
12.10.40	Blenheim		Ewhurst Place, Ewhurst
12.10.40	Hurricane		Coghurst Woods, Guestling
25.10.40	Spitfire		Stonelink Farm, Brede
25.10.40	"		Pickdick Farm, Brede
25.10.40	M/schmitt 109	D5	Bardown Farm, Ticehurst
25.10.40	"		Wall Hse Fm, Camber
25.10.40	"		Lidham Hill Farm, Guestling
25.10.40	Hurricane	D6	Barn Field, Brightling
30.10.40	Spitfire		Hr. Wilting Fm, Crowhurst
30.10.40	"		Great Dixter, Northiam
9.11.40	Wellington		In sea at Cliffend, Fairlight
11.11.40	M/schmitt 109		Blackwall Bridge, Peasmarsh
28.11.40	"		Stocks Cottage, Udimore
1.12.40	Spitfire	D7	Tolhurst Fm, Ticehurst
16.12.40	Blenheim		Fairlight
17.12.40	Wellington		Military Road, Rye
22.12.40	Heinkel 111		Underwood Hse, Etchingham

BEXHILL MUNICIPAL BOROUGH

28.7.40	Junkers 88		Buckholt Fm, nr. Sidley
27.12.40	Spitfire		Freezelands Fm, Bexhill

BOGNOR REGIS URBAN DISTRICT

10.9.40	Spitfire		Felpham Golf Course
15.11.40	M/schmitt 109		Felpham Beach

BRIGHTON COUNTY BOROUGH   Nil

BURGESS HILL URBAN DISTRICT   Nil

CHAILEY RURAL DISTRICT

4.7.40	Hurricane		Southease, Rodmell
29.9.40	"		Longridge Fm, Wivelsfield
1.10.40	M/schmitt 109		Balmer Down, Falmer
12.10.40	Spitfiire		Iford Farm, Iford
25.10.40	M/schmitt 109		Harveys Cross Fm, Iford
27.10.40	Hurricane		Sewells Farm, Barcombe
28.10.40	M/schmitt 109		Townings Farm, Chailey
22.11.40	Dornier 17		South Heighton
1.12.40	Hurricane		N.Camp Meadow, Falmer

CHANCTONBURY RURAL DISTRICT

20.7.40	Hurricane		Amberley
16.8.40	M/schmitt 110		Lee Farm, Rackham
16.8.40	Heinkel 111		Annington Fm, Bramber
18.8.40	Hurricane		Mare Hill, Pulborough
4.9.40	M/schmitt 110		Church Farm, Washington
4.9.40	"		Toat Farm, nr. Pulborough
4.9.40	"		Strivens Farm, Steyning
9.9.40	M/schmitt 109		Charity Farm, Storrington
1.10.40	Spitfire	B13	Heatenthorn Fm, Henfield
30.10.40	Hurricane		Wild Brooks, Amberley
1.11.40	Junkers 88		Greyfriars Rd, Storrington

CHICHESTER MUNICIPAL BOROUGH

18.8.40	Junkers 87	A23	West Broyle, Chichester

CHICHESTER RURAL DISTRICT

4.9.39	Anson	A1	Thorney Island Creek

Date	Aircraft		Location
19.9.39	Gladiator		Nr Tangmere Airfield
19.9.39	"		" "
12.10.39	Tutor		Near Sidlesham
15.11.39	Blenheim		On approach to Tangmere
7.2.40	Anson		West Wittering
7.6.40	Spitfire		Three miles SE Tangmere
17.6.40	Bombay		East Dean
7.7.40	Hurricane		Lidsey Bridge, Bersted
9.7.40	"		Fontwell
11.7.40	Heinkel 111	A2	East Beach, Selsey
16.7.40	Swordfish		West Harting
21.7.40	M/schmitt 110		Home Farm, Goodwood
22.7.40	Hurricane		Morrells Farm, Pagham
12.8.40	Junkers 88		Horse Past. Fm, Rowlands Csl
13.8.40	Hurricane		Eartham
13.8.40	Junkers 88	A3	Great Ham Fm, Selsey
15.8.40	Hurricane	A4	Greenwood Fm, Sidlesham
15.8.40	"		Near Selsey
15.8.40	Junkers 88		Great Ham Fm, Selsey
15.8.40	"		Woodmancote, Westbourne
16.8.40	M/schmitt 110		East Dean
16.8.40	"	A5	Shopwyke Hse, Nr Tangmere
16.8.40	Hurricane	A6	Manor Farm, Chidham
16.8.40	"		Woodgate, Aldingbourne
16.8.40	Junkers 87	A7	Honor Farm, Sidlesham
16.8.40	"	A8	Bowley Farm, S.Mundham
16.8.40	"	A9	Alongside B2145, Selsey
18.8.40	"	A10	Fishbourne Creek, Bosham
18.8.40	Hurricane		Summer Lane, Nyetimber
18.8.40	Junkers 87	A11	Cut Mill, West Ashling
18.8.40	"	A12	North Barn, Chidham
18.8.40	Spitfire		Elmer Sands, Middleton
19.8.40	"	A13	Norton, nr. Selsey
19.8.40	"		Colworth Farm, Merston
21.8.40	Junkers 88	A14	Marsh Farm, Earnley
24.8.40	Blenheim		In Bracklesham Bay
26.8.40	Hurricane		Warren Down, Forestside
26.8.40	"	A15	Ratham Mill, W.Ashling
26.8.40	"		Birdham
26.8.40	"		West Wittering
26.8.40	Heinkel 111	A16	On beach, Bracklesham Bay
9.9.40	Spitfire		Crocker Hill, Boxgrove
9.9.40	Junkers 88		Pagham Beach, Pagham
21.9.40	"	A17	Mudberry Farm, Bosham
25.9.40	Blenheim		Stockers Sands, W. Wittering
5.10.40	Shark		Green Lane, Slindon
5.10.40	Hurricane		Woodhorn Fm, Aldingbourne
7.10.40	"		Seas Farm, Slindon
7.10.40	"		Eartham Farm, Eartham
8.10.40	Heinkel 111		Stansted Park, Stoughton
8.10.40	Blenheim		Chidham
30.10.40	"		South Bersted
1.11.40	Hurricane		Liphook Game Fm, Stoughton
1.11.40	M/schmitt 109	A18	Mapsons Farm, Sidlesham
7.11.40	Hurricane		Earnley Mill, Birdham
12.11.40	Beaufighter		Tangmere
13.11.40	Blenheim		Thorney Island
15.11.40	Spitfire		Birdham
20.11.40	Junkers 88	A19	Stocks Ln, East Wittering
23.11.40	Boston		Ford
23.11.40	Blenheim		Near Tangmere
30.11.40	Hurricane	A20	Donnington
2.12.40	M/schmitt 109	A21	Off Pilsey Island
6.12.40	Blenheim		Near Thorney Island
8.12.40	Hurricane		Tangmere
11.12.40	Spitfire		Westhampnett
19.12.40	Wellington		Pilsey Sands
29.12.40	Hurricane		Selhurst Park, East Dean

CUCKFIELD RURAL DISTRICT

Date	Aircraft		Location
26.4.40	Hurricane		Near Three Bridges
30.8.40	Heinkel 111		Ashfold X-ways, Lr Beeding
9.9.40	Junkers 88		Court House Fm, Barcombe
9.9.40	Hurricane	B10	Saddlescombe Fm, Newtimber
9.9.40	"		Cambridgeshire F, Falmer
10.9.40	Dornier 17		Lr Sheriff's Cotts, W Hoathly
30.9.40	M/schmitt 109		Cinderhill Farm, Horsted Keyne
4.10.40	Hurricane	B11	Ockley Manor Farm, Keymer
4.10.40	"		Great Bentley Fm, Cuckfield
8.10.40	Junkers 88		Toovies Farm, Worth
10.10.40	Spitfire	B12	Old Dyke Rly Stn, Poynings
25.10.40	Hurricane		High Beeches Golf Course
30.10.40	Beaufighter		Balcombe Place, Balcombe
11.12.40	Gypsy Moth		Twineham

CUCKFIELD URBAN DISTRICT   Nil

EASTBOURNE COUNTY BOROUGH

Date	Aircraft		Location
16.8.40	M/schmitt 110	C1	Aldro School, Meads
30.9.40	M/schmitt 109	C2	Alongside A259, E.Dean
30.9.40	"		Langney
17.11.40	Spitfire		Near Eastbourne

EAST GRINSTEAD URBAN DISTRICT

Date	Aircraft	Location
26.8.40	Spitfire	Near East Grinstead
15.9.40	Hurricane	Gulledges Fm, Imberhorne
27.9.40	Junkers 88	N.End Lodge, E. Grinstead

HAILSHAM RURAL DISTRICT

Date	Aircraft		Location
9.3.39	Anson		Near Wilmington
13.3.40	Lysander	C3	Marshfoot Lane, Hailsham
13.3.40	Hurricane		Laughton
17.7.40	Spitfire	C4	Hempstead Lane, Hailsham
12.8.40	M/schmitt 109		Mays Farm, Selmeston
16.8.40	Spitfire		Dower House, Possingworth
29.8.40	M/schmitt 109	C5	Near Pevensey Radar Stn
9.9.40	Hurricane	C6	Squires Field, Pevensey
13.9.40	"	C7	Perryland Wood, Lr Dicker
21.9.40	Lysander		Near Ripe Church
27.9.40	M/schmitt 109		Lr Mays Farm, Selmeston
27.9.40	M/schmitt 110		Nr May Garland Inn, Horam
27.9.40	"	C8	Mill Rd, Hailsham
27.9.40	"		Coppice Fm, Three Cups
27.9.40	Hurricane	C9	Station Rd, Hailsham
30.9.40	M/schmitt 109	C10	Rockhouse Bank, Normans Bay
7.10.40	Spitfire		Court Farm, Lullington
20.10.40	M/schmitt 109		Court Wood, Waldron
27.10.40	Spitfire	C11	Battle Road, Hailsham
30.10.40	Hurricane		Blackford Fm, Herstmonceux
7.11.40	Magister	C12	Ersham Farm, Hailsham
1.12.40	Hurricane		Whiligh Wood, East Hoathly
7.12.40	Spitfire	C13	Foreshore, Pevensey Bay
22.12.40	"		Old Park Farm, Arlington
22.12.40	Wellington	C14	Boreham Street
22.12.40	"		Mill Lane, Lullington

HASTINGS COUNTY BOROUGH

Date	Aircraft	Location
9.9.40	Anson	Off Fairlight
27.10.40	Hurricane	Hollington
4.11.40	"	Hastings

HORSHAM RURAL DISTRICT

27.10.39	Lysander	Broadbridge Heath
21.4.40	Hurricane	Cowfold
27.6.40	Gladiator	Lower Beeding
14.8.40	Whitley	Ifield, Crawley
9.9.40	M/schmitt 109	Roman Gate, Rudgwick
9.9.40	Junkers 88	Newells Farm, Nuthurst
24.10.40	Hurricane	Cricklegate, Shipley
27.10.40	"	Christs Hospital, Itchingfield
29.10.40	M/schmitt 109	Plummers Plain
23.12.40	Hart	Marlands, Itchingfield
24.12.40	Tiger Moth	Railway S. of Three Bridges

HORSHAM RURAL DISTRICT   Nil

HOVE MUNICIPAL BOROUGH

30.8.40	Hurricane	B1	Off Portland Road, Hove
10.10.40	Spitfire	B2	Fallowfield Crescent, Hove

LEWES MUNICIPAL BOROUGH

28.8.40	Gotha 145	Lewes Racecourse
11.9.40	M/schmitt 109	Houndean Bottom, Lewes
27.9.40	Spitfire	Lewes Racecourse

LITTLEHAMPTON URBAN DISTRICT

18.8.40	Junkers 87	Ham Manor Golf Course
26.8.40	Heinkel 111	Hellyers Farm, Wick

MIDHURST RURAL DISTRICT

13.8.40	Hurricane	Cocking Down
13.8.40	"	Northend Farm, Stedham
13.8.40	Junkers 88	Phillis Wood, Treyford
24.11.40	Whitley	Elsted Manor Fm, Treyford
12.12.40	Gypsy Moth	Halfway Bridge, Lodsworth
24.12.40	Magister	Filtsham Farm, Cocking

NEWHAVEN URBAN DISTRICT

29.9.40	Hurricane	New Road, Newhaven

PETWORTH RURAL DISTRICT

16.8.40	Heinkel 111	Upper Frithfold Fm, Kirdford
30.9.40	M/schmit 109	Roundhurst Fm, Northchapel
11.12.40	Tiger Moth	Petworth

PORTSLADE URBAN DISTRICT

21.3.40	Blenheim	B3	South Downs, N. of Mile Oak
10.10.40	Spitfire	B4	Jubilee Field, Portslade
24.11.40	Whitley	B5	Applesham Way, Portslade

RYE MUNICIPAL BOROUGH   Nil

SEAFORD URBAN DISTRICT   Nil

SHOREHAM BY SEA URBAN DISTRICT

19.7.40	Hurricane	Shoreham Airport

13.8.40	M/schmitt 109	B6	New Salts Farm, nr Airport
15.9.40	Spitfire		Shoreham Airport
30.9.40	"		" "
9.12.40	Beaufighter		" "

SOUTHWICK URBAN DISTRICT   Nil

UCKFIELD RURAL DISTRICT

17.7.40	Lysander		Near Forest Row
24.7.40	Spitfire		Great Bainden Fm, Mayfield
15.8.40	M/schmitt 109	D9	Lightlands Farm, Frant
15.8.40	M/schmitt 110	D10	Bletchinglye Farm, Rotherfield
23.8.40	Hurricane		Hunts Farm, Withyham
30.8.40	Heinkel 111		Roy Hill, Blackboys
4.9.40	Spitfire		Culvers Farm, Hartfield
4.9.40	M/schmitt 110	D11	Little Butts, Cousley Wood
6.9.40	Spitfire		Howbourne Fm, Hadlow Dn
9.9.40	M/schmitt 109	D12	Knowle Farm, Mayfield
11.9.40	Hurricane		Nr Withyham Post Office
11.9.40	"		Lake Street Farm, Mayfield
11.9.40	Spitfire		Parsonage Farm, Fletching
11.9.40	M/schmitt 109	D14	Foxhole Lane, Wadhurst
15.9.40	Dornier 17	D15	Nr Bicycle Arms, Rotherfield
15.9.40	M/schmitt 109		Lodge Wood, Isfield
27.9.40	Spitfire	D16	Batts Wood, Mayfield
27.9.40	Hurricane		Holwych Farm, Hartfield
27.9.40	M/schmitt 110		Chelwood Gate, Ashdown Forest
30.9.40	Hurricane		Tablehurst Farm, Forest Row
30.9.40	M/schmitt 109		Bell Lane, Nutley
3.10.40	Blenheim		Broadstone Warren, Forest Row
6.10.40	Dornier 17	D17	Snape, Wadhurst
7.10.40	M/schmitt 109	D18	Mayfield Flats, Cross in Hand
15.10.40	"		Owles Castle, Cousley Wood
26.10.40	Hurricane		Greenhouse Farm, Rotherfield
8.11.40	"	D19	Xaverian College, Mayfield
8.11.40	"		Pound Farm, Withyham
21.11.40	"		Ham Farm, Groombridge
21.12.40	Spitfire		Horsegrove Farm, Rotherfield

WORTHING MUNICIPAL BOROUGH

16.8.40	Heinkel 111	Honeysuckle Ln, H.Salvington
4.9.40	Hurricane	Goring
4.9.40	M/schmitt 110	High Salvington

WORTHING RURAL DISTRICT

30.7.40	Hampden	B7	Mill Hill, near Shoreham
18.8.40	Spitfire		Norway Farm, Rustington
4.9.40	M/schmitt 110	B8	Mill Hill, near Shoreham
4.9.40	"		Patching
13.10.40	Blenheim	B9	Near Lancing College

There were more than 300 incidents over Sussex and immediately offshore representing about 120 German losses and 180 British. These events claimed the lives of 143 German aircrew with 147 taken Prisoners of War and 61 British aircrew died. Before the end of hostilities a total of 935 aircraft were to crash in the county, made up as follows:

666 British, 102 American, 167 German

In addition, 310 members of the civilian population lost their lives through enemy action in Sussex during 1940.

Middleton Press

Easebourne Lane, Midhurst, W Sussex. GU29 9AZ Tel: 01730 813169 Fax: 01730 812601
Email: enquiries@middletonpress.fsnet.co.uk *If books are not available from your*
local transport stockist, order direct with cheque, Visa or Mastercard, post free UK.

BRANCH LINES
Branch Line to Allhallows
Branch Line to Alton
Branch Lines around Ascot
Branch Line to Ashburton
Branch Lines around Bodmin
Branch Line to Bude
Branch Lines around Canterbury
Branch Lines around Chard & Yeovil
Branch Line to Cheddar
Branch Lines around Cromer
Branch Lines to East Grinstead
Branch Lines of East London
Branch Lines to Effingham Junction
Branch Lines around Exmouth
Branch Lines to Falmouth, Helston & St. Ives
Branch Line to Fairford
Branch Lines around Gosport
Branch Line to Hayling
Branch Lines to Henley, Windsor & Marlow
Branch Line to Hawkhurst
Branch Lines around Huntingdon
Branch Line to Ilfracombe
Branch Line to Kingsbridge
Branch Line to Kingswear
Branch Line to Lambourn
Branch Lines to Launceston & Princetown
Branch Lines to Longmoor
Branch Line to Looe
Branch Line to Lyme Regis
Branch Lines around Midhurst
Branch Line to Minehead
Branch Line to Moretonhampstead
Branch Lines to Newport (IOW)
Branch Lines to Newquay
Branch Lines around North Woolwich
Branch Line to Padstow
Branch Lines around Plymouth
Branch Lines to Seaton and Sidmouth
Branch Lines around Sheerness
Branch Line to Shrewsbury
Branch Line to Swanage *updated*
Branch Line to Tenterden
Branch Lines around Tiverton
Branch Lines to Torrington
Branch Line to Upwell
Branch Lines of West London
Branch Lines around Weymouth
Branch Lines around Wimborne
Branch Lines around Wisbech

NARROW GAUGE
Branch Line to Lynton
Branch Lines around Portmadoc 1923-46
Branch Lines around Porthmadog 1954-94
Branch Line to Southwold
Douglas to Port Erin
Douglas to Peel
Kent Narrow Gauge
Northern France Narrow Gauge
Romneyrail
Southern France Narrow Gauge
Sussex Narrow Gauge
Surrey Narrow Gauge
Swiss Narrow Gauge
Two-Foot Gauge Survivors
Vivarais Narrow Gauge

SOUTH COAST RAILWAYS
Ashford to Dover

Bournemouth to Weymouth
Brighton to Worthing
Eastbourne to Hastings
Hastings to Ashford
Portsmouth to Southampton
Ryde to Ventnor
Southampton to Bournemouth

SOUTHERN MAIN LINES
Basingstoke to Salisbury
Bromley South to Rochester
Crawley to Littlehampton
Dartford to Sittingbourne
East Croydon to Three Bridges
Epsom to Horsham
Exeter to Barnstaple
Exeter to Tavistock
Faversham to Dover
London Bridge to East Croydon
Orpington to Tonbridge
Tonbridge to Hastings
Salisbury to Yeovil
Sittingbourne to Ramsgate
Swanley to Ashford
Tavistock to Plymouth
Three Bridges to Brighton
Victoria to Bromley South
Victoria to East Croydon
Waterloo to Windsor
Waterloo to Woking
Woking to Portsmouth
Woking to Southampton
Yeovil to Exeter

EASTERN MAIN LINES
Barking to Southend
Ely to Kings Lynn
Ely to Norwich
Fenchurch Street to Barking
Ilford to Shenfield
Ipswich to Saxmundham
Liverpool Street to Ilford
Saxmundham to Yarmouth
Tilbury Loop

WESTERN MAIN LINES
Didcot to Banbury
Didcot to Swindon
Ealing to Slough
Exeter to Newton Abbot
Newton Abbot to Plymouth
Newbury to Westbury
Paddington to Ealing
Paddington to Princes Risborough
Plymouth to St. Austell
Princes Risborough to Banbury
Reading to Didcot
Slough to Newbury
St. Austell to Penzance
Swindon to Bristol
Taunton to Exeter
Westbury to Taunton

MIDLAND MAIN LINES
Euston to Harrow & Wealdstone
St. Pancras to St. Albans

COUNTRY RAILWAY ROUTES
Abergavenny to Merthyr
Andover to Southampton
Bath to Evercreech Junction
Bath Green Park to Bristol
Burnham to Evercreech Junction
Cheltenham to Andover
Croydon to East Grinstead
Didcot to Winchester
East Kent Light Railway
Fareham to Salisbury
Guildford to Redhill
Reading to Basingstoke
Reading to Guildford
Redhill to Ashford
Salisbury to Westbury
Stratford upon Avon to Cheltenham
Strood to Paddock Wood
Taunton to Barnstaple
Wenford Bridge to Fowey
Westbury to Bath
Woking to Alton
Yeovil to Dorchester

GREAT RAILWAY ERAS
Ashford from Steam to Eurostar
Clapham Junction 50 years of change
Festiniog in the Fifties
Festiniog in the Sixties
Festiniog 50 years of enterprise
Isle of Wight Lines 50 years of change
Railways to Victory 1944-46
Return to Blaenau 1970-82
SECR Centenary album
Talyllyn 50 years of change
Yeovil 50 years of change

LONDON SUBURBAN RAILWAYS
Caterham and Tattenham Corner
Charing Cross to Dartford
Clapham Jn. to Beckenham Jn.
Crystal Palace (HL) & Catford Loop
East London Line
Finsbury Park to Alexandra Palace
Holbourn Viaduct to Lewisham
Kingston and Hounslow Loops
Lewisham to Dartford
Lines around Wimbledon
Liverpool Street to Chingford
London Bridge to Addiscombe
Mitcham Junction Lines
North London Line
South London Line
West Croydon to Epsom
West London Line
Willesden Junction to Richmond
Wimbledon to Beckenham
Wimbledon to Epsom

STEAMING THROUGH
Steaming through Cornwall
Steaming through the Isle of Wight
Steaming through Kent
Steaming through West Hants

TRAMWAY CLASSICS
Aldgate & Stepney Tramways
Barnet & Finchley Tramways

Bath Tramways
Brighton's Tramways
Bristol's Tramways
Burton & Ashby Tramways
Camberwell & W.Norwood Tramways
Clapham & Streatham Tramways
Croydon's Tramways
Dover's Tramways
East Ham & West Ham Tramways
Edgware and Willesden Tramways
Eltham & Woolwich Tramways
Embankment & Waterloo Tramways
Enfield & Wood Green Tramways
Exeter & Taunton Tramways
Greenwich & Dartford Tramways
Hammersmith & Hounslow Tramways
Hampstead & Highgate Tramways
Hastings Tramways
Holborn & Finsbury Tramways
Ilford & Barking Tramways
Kingston & Wimbledon Tramways
Lewisham & Catford Tramways
Liverpool Tramways 1. Eastern Routes
Liverpool Tramways 2. Southern Routes
Liverpool Tramways 3. Northern Routes
Maidstone & Chatham Tramways
Margate to Ramsgate
North Kent Tramways
Norwich Tramways
Reading Tramways
Seaton & Eastbourne Tramways
Shepherds Bush & Uxbridge Tramways
Southend-on-sea Tramways
Southwark & Deptford Tramways
Stamford Hill Tramways
Twickenham & Kingston Tramways
Victoria & Lambeth Tramways
Waltham Cross & Edmonton Tramways
Walthamstow & Leyton Tramways
Wandsworth & Battersea Tramways

TROLLEYBUS CLASSICS
Croydon Trolleybuses
Derby Trolleybuses
Hastings Trolleybuses
Huddersfield Trolleybuses
Maidstone Trolleybuses
Portsmouth Trolleybuses
Woolwich & Dartford Trolleybuses

WATERWAY ALBUMS
Kent and East Sussex Waterways
London to Portsmouth Waterway
West Sussex Waterways

MILITARY BOOKS
Battle over Portsmouth
Battle over Sussex 1940
Bombers over Sussex 1943-45
Bognor at War
Military Defence of West Sussex
Military Signals from the South Coast
Secret Sussex Resistance
Surrey Home Guard

OTHER RAILWAY BOOKS
Index to all Middleton Press station
Industrial Railways of the South-East
South Eastern & Chatham Railways
London Chatham & Dover Railway
London Termini - Past and Proposed
War on the Line (SR 1939-45)

BIOGRAPHY
Garraway Father & Son